Out of the Shadows
The role of social workers in disasters

Other books you may be interested in:

Social Work and Covid-19: Lessons for Education and Practice
Edited by Denise Turner   ISBN 9781913453619

Digital Connection in Health and Social Work: Perspectives from Covid-19
Edited by Denise Turner and Michael Fanner   ISBN 9781914171925

*The Anti-racist Social Worker: Stories of Activism by Social Care
and Allied Health Professionals*
Edited by Tanya Moore and Glory Simango   ISBN 9781914171413

Anti-racism in Social Work Practice
Edited by Angie Bartoli   ISBN 9781909330139

Our titles are also available in a range of electronic formats. To order, or for details of our bulk discounts, please go to our website www.criticalpublishing.com or contact our distributor Ingram Publisher Services, telephone 01752 202301 or email NBNi.Cservs@ingramcontent.com

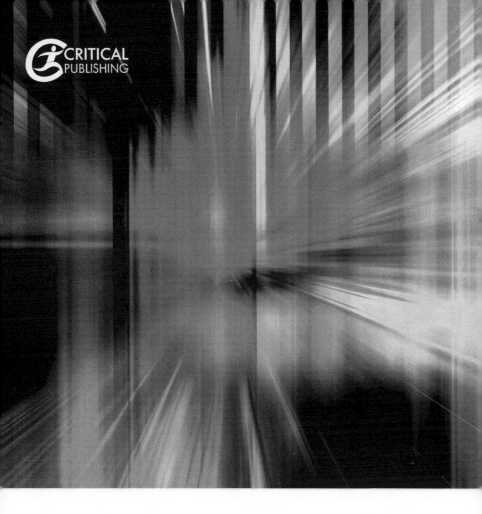

Out of the Shadows
The role of social workers in disasters

Edited by Angie Bartoli,
Maris Stratulis and Rebekah Pierre

BASW
England
The professional association for
social work and social workers

First published in 2022 by Critical Publishing Ltd

British Library Cataloguing in Publication Data
A CIP record for this book is available from the British Library

ISBN: 9781915080073

This book is also available in the following e-book formats:
EPUB ISBN: 9781915080080
Adobe e-book ISBN: 9781915080097

Cover and text design by Out of House Ltd
Project management by Newgen Publishing UK
Printed and bound in Great Britain by 4edge, Essex

Critical Publishing
3 Connaught Road
St Albans
AL3 5RX

www.criticalpublishing.com

Printed on FSC accredited paper

BASW
England
The professional association for
social work and social workers

The Social Workers' Benevolent Trust

All royalties from sales of this book are going to the Social Workers' Benevolent Trust. Established as an independent charity in 1971 on the initiative of the British Association of Social Workers (Charity No 262889), it remains independent with its own trustees and is the UK's only charity dedicated to helping social workers when times are difficult. The Trust offers financial help to social workers and their dependants in times of hardship, for example when experiencing sickness, bereavement, family difficulties or sudden catastrophe. It is a small charity with limited funds, and it aims to provide grants that will make a tangible difference to the applicants. For more information about the Trust visit www.swbt.org/about-swbt.

Contents

About the editors

Angie Bartoli

My interest in disaster work stems from my volunteer work in Romania in the early 1990s, after the fall of Ceauşescu, which exposed the overcrowded and inhumane conditions in the orphanages. I was hugely impacted by the experience – the sights, sounds, smells and resilience of a generation robbed of a childhood and hidden away in the most appalling conditions. Not long after this, in 1994 I qualified as a social worker and have worked with children and families within the statutory and voluntary sectors as a practitioner and manager. I worked for a period of time with the Department of Education and was a training manager for a Local Safeguarding Children Board. I am now a social work educator working at Nottingham Trent University and gained my professional doctorate in 2016. Since becoming the vice-chair for the British Association of Social Workers (BASW) England, I have been involved in the BASW England campaign to raise awareness and formalise the important role social workers play in disaster recovery and I have had the privilege of meeting a number of colleagues involved in social work in disasters and those with lived experience, many of whom have kindly contributed to this book

Maris Stratulis

I am a registered social worker and have a Master of Laws in Human Rights from the University of Nottingham. I have worked in a variety of strategic social work leadership roles, both in the UK and overseas, including working for Save the Children in Bosnia Herzegovina as a child protection adviser and in other roles in Malaysia and Papua New Guinea. I have worked for the Refugee Council as the manager for the Panel of Unaccompanied Refugee Children and as director for the British Red Cross Nottinghamshire, and have managed children in need, safeguarding and children in care services. As such, I have been instrumental in the development of strategic partnerships, integrated leadership, service planning, policy development and commissioning with a strong focus on co-production. I have also held a variety of children and adult services roles in local authorities in London and the East Midlands. My passion and interest in disaster work is based on personal experience of the impact of such events, including the Hillsborough disaster, Kosovo refugee programme, co-ordination of emergency responses and working within the context of a post-war environment. As the national director (England) for BASW, I am committed to working 'with' people with lived experiences and ensuring the legacies of those who have died and those who have been directly affected by disaster are heard.

Rebekah Pierre

I have worked extensively with children and families in settings where disasters are common, including overseas in Uganda, India and Chile; the latter included working with the United Nations ministry of education in rural Tarapacá, where earthquakes were frequent, and the land is heavily impacted by climate change. My most recent experience of disaster settings was during the Covid-19 pandemic, where I worked as a frontline social worker in an inner-London child protection team. As an editor of this work, I bring the dual perspective of being a social work practitioner, as well as somebody with lived experience of the care system. I have written extensively around the manifestation of trauma within the body, and ways in which practitioners can help children to reconnect with their embodied selves – which may have been home to abuse or suffering – through creative methods. Having been through the process of sharing my lived experience through autoethnographic works, I am passionate about encouraging others to share their story in a way in which they have complete ownership – something I drew upon throughout this book. I am currently a professional officer at BASW England.

Foreword

In June 2018, on an uncharacteristically sunny day in England, I attended a symposium held at Durham University about Social Work in Disasters. The symposium was held in a large room set out in what is known as a cabaret layout with delegates seated at large tables for six to eight people, with Durham University master's students acting as facilitators on each table. Our first activity centred on a discussion, sharing our own personal or professional experience of being involved in a disaster – either natural or caused by humans. At first most of us, including myself, confessed to being 'lucky' enough not to have been touched by a disaster. As the discussion progressed and we collectively developed a more nuanced and shared understanding of what a *disaster* might actually mean, one by one, our memories were jogged. We recalled experiences of working in warzones, orphanages in post-political revolution countries, or surviving hurricanes, earthquakes and rail crashes. Curiously, we acknowledged that these events were disasters and talking about them took us back to the associated fear, smells and sights, yet intellectually we had not categorised them as such.

As the day progressed, the warm weather drew delegates outside during coffee breaks where conversations and debates continued. I was unable to pull myself away from other social workers and those with lived experience, like a magnet, drawn to their stories and their involvement in disasters. I returned late to the main hall of the symposium after each break, nodding a silent apology. It was during one of these breaks that I realised that, for most of the delegates, this was the first time they had been invited to share their narrative and, more importantly, a platform where their words were welcomed and listened to. And so, the idea of capturing these often unknown and unheard powerful stories in a book emerged.

Little did we know when we were planning this book, shaping the chapters, and sending call outs for contributions, that we would find ourselves in the midst of a global pandemic. The process of editing this book has been slower than expected. Delays were inevitable due to the pandemic, which for some contributors rekindled feelings of loss, fear and isolation, and so the writing or telling of their stories took longer. Our ways of living and working changed forever.

On a personal level, I lost my dad to Covid-19. He came to the UK in the 1950s as a Sicilian migrant. He settled in the UK, working hard until retirement. He was quirky, stubborn and quick to share an opinion. He was also fun, making others laugh without realising why, and he introduced me to the beautiful game – football. He was 92 years of age, living in a care home and ironically tested positive on the day he was due to have his Covid-19 vaccination. I am grateful for the long and happy life Dad had – but he did not deserve to end his life alone, on a ventilator in an unfamiliar hospital. Dad is one of many thousands of people who have been robbed of a dignified ending.

We are truly indebted to those who have contributed to this book. Their willingness to gift their time, to recount their story, has been humbling and a true privilege. Ongoing public enquiries meant that some contributors felt they could no longer share their story, which of course I understand and respect. Their time will come.

Finding the *right* time to conclude this book has been difficult. As I write these words, the world's leaders congregate to attend the COP26 Climate Change Conference in Glasgow to address what arguably is the largest scale global disaster we have ever faced – saving our planet.

Disasters are ongoing and relentless with no neat conclusion. New catastrophes and events continue to impact on us, provoking memories and forming fresh images in our minds and hearts forever.

Dedication

This book is dedicated to social workers who have worked tirelessly and unnoticed in disasters, to those who have experienced unspeakable loss, and in memory of colleagues, friends and loved ones who are no longer with us.

Special thanks

To Brenda, for her patience, encouragement, and of course, proof-reading skills.

Angie Bartoli

CHAPTER 1

INTRODUCTION

Introduction to the book

Social work has often been described as the fifth emergency service; long after our deeply valued colleagues from health, fire and police services have been and gone, social workers stick around to pick up the pieces. Other emergency services have more tangible outcomes; in some, but not all cases, the human body may be nursed to good health. Homes may be rebuilt. Justice may be served. Social work, on the other hand is a messier science. Traumatic life events cannot be erased, nor is there any guarantee that social-emotional well-being can be restored to what it once was. Our work goes beyond the immediate and into the unknown realm of long-term, often with no definite timeline.

Our work may be less measurable, and often less visible than allied colleagues, but is certainly no less valuable. In this chapter, we aim to highlight both the role and importance of social workers in a host of disaster situations, referring to those which have occurred in an England-context within living memory. The very concept and definition of a disaster will also be explored, including natural, accidental, terrorist-related and within a pandemic.

The chapter will also explore how societal factors and intersectionality place minoritised groups at higher risk of experiencing, and being further impacted by, disasters. The need for such a book as this will also be discussed, at a time in history where, sadly, disasters are more and more likely to occur. The role of the British Association of Social Workers (BASW) following historic and current disasters will also be explored, as will the purpose of BASW continual professional development guidance.

To provide readers with a compass to traverse the rich survivor/social worker-led content of the book, the chapter will conclude with a brief structure of the proceeding chapters. The voices of survivors are the golden thread which runs throughout – these are deeply moving, and we recommend taking the time and space necessary to reflect on these in all their fullness as you progress through the book.

As a profession, social work has a long history in supporting and working with individuals, groups and communities affected by disasters. Despite this, social workers rarely receive public recognition for their role (Dominelli, 2015). When disaster strikes, the vital role of the social worker is often overlooked. The emergency blue light services and the medical profession are the most visible, arriving at the scene almost immediately. However, the involvement of social workers goes beyond the initial crisis as the impact of disasters have long-term consequences such as displacement, loss, psychological trauma and survivor guilt. These traumatic impacts highlight the importance of social work in the recovery phase of disasters. While supporting communities in the immediate aftermath is crucial, recovery is often a long process. The initial help from volunteers and fundraising can come to an end but social workers remain involved to provide ongoing crucial services and support.

It has been argued that globally, social workers play an integral role in disaster responses and have the potential of bringing 'a unique understanding to the disaster field by underscoring values of our profession and giving attention to the oppressed and disadvantaged populations' (Bauwens and Naturale, 2017, p 99). Social work education is such that our skills, knowledge and expertise are critically valuable in an emergency, as well as in post-disaster recovery work. Historically, within an England context, this has been evidenced in the Kegworth air disaster and the Hillsborough football tragedy. More recently this has included the Manchester Arena terrorist attack, the Grenfell Tower fire and the current Covid-19 pandemic.

Disasters can have significant consequences for individuals and communities, and we are aware that individuals involved in such horrifying events have valued the support of social workers in many ways and acknowledge the difference it made to them, their families, and communities.

What is a disaster?

Before this book was written, we invited both those with lived experience and social workers to contribute in whatever form felt right for them, whether through writing, spoken word, poetry or art. Early on, we noticed that we were receiving startlingly different responses; some accounts referred to national disasters, such as terrorist attacks, pandemics or natural emergencies. Others referred to events which impacted on more intimate networks, such as suicide or illness. The term 'disaster' seemed to mean different things to different people. Certainly, dictionary definitions existed, but the term seemed so subjective. As we slowly collated the stories, common threads appeared despite the diversity of events referred to; invariably, the disaster in question, whether on a national or personal scale, was something that crumbled the very foundations of people's lives. Amid the uncertainty of the term, one thing is crystal clear – if someone describes their lived experience as a 'disaster', then it meets the criteria.

Similar to our contributors, the literature indicates that there are a number of ways that disasters have been defined and much of this appears to relate to whether the definition focuses on the cause of the disaster or the impact on individuals and communities (Alston et al, 2019). Despite this a disaster is 'characterised by urgency, uncertainty and panic' (Yanay and Benjamin, 2005, p 265) and largely defined as 'sudden unforeseen events with natural, technological or social causes that lead to destruction, loss and damage' (Al-Dahash et al, 2016, p 1192). Many writers differentiate between 'natural' disasters like an earthquake or storm as opposed to those caused by humans, such as an act of terrorism or conflict. Some argue that 'natural' disasters have a human component due to the cause being linked with climate change, such as flooding (Alston et al, 2019).

Two major international organisations that deal with disasters on a global scale, the Red Cross and the World Health Organization, define disasters in a similar way. The World Health Organization (WHO, 2020e) describes a disaster as '*A serious disruption of the functioning of a community or a society causing widespread human, material, economic or environmental losses that exceed the ability of the affected community or society to cope using its own resources*'.

For the purposes of this book, we will be adopting the International Federation of Red Cross and Red Crescent Societies (IFRC) definition, as it includes disasters that have human origins and explicitly identifies vulnerability as a significant factor, which fits well with social work values and practice.

Disaster defined

The IFRC (2020) defines a disaster as:

> *a sudden, calamitous event that seriously disrupts the functioning of a community or society and causes human, material and economic or environmental loses that exceed the community's or society's ability to cope using its own resource. Though often caused by nature, disasters can have human origins.*

It goes on to define disasters as an equation that occurs when a hazard impacts on vulnerable people.

VULNERABILITY + HAZARD = DISASTER

Who is impacted by disasters?

The impact of disasters and those affected tends to mirror societal oppression (Willett, 2019). Research informs us that human disaster figures such as the number of those deceased or displaced are not usually disaggregated by gender, age or other socio-economic factors, which leaves us with a significant gap in our understanding of the impact on different groups and communities (Seballos et al, 2011). However, we do know that those living in marginalised communities and those who experience injustices and discrimination are further impacted by disasters. Consequently, those already vulnerable are more severely and disproportionately affected (Willett, 2019; Yanay and Benjamin, 2005).

The impact of disasters can affect individuals at different stages of the life course. Older adults are more likely to be impacted due to age-related changes, physical illness or mental health issues (Ellor and Mayo, 2018). For example, restricted movement can render individuals more prone to injury or death (Barusch, 2011). According to Age International (2018), 26 million older people are affected by natural disasters every year, yet only 0.2 per cent of appeals for human relief target older people. Similarly, children are particularly impacted and less equipped to deal with disasters. This is mainly due to their physiological, emotional and social development. They are even more severely impacted when they are part of a low-income family or live in poor housing conditions (Seballos et al, 2011).

As well as age, women and girls are also further impacted by disasters. The work conducted by Bradshaw and Fordham (2013) demonstrates that disasters have a gendered impact, where men and women experience disasters differently. For example, in the December 2004 tsunami in the Indian Ocean, the largest number of people who lost their lives were women and girls. Yet the 'second wave of horror' affecting the women is not from the immediate disaster but gender inequalities resulting in an increase of rape, domestic violence and physical abuse against women and children (Pittaway et al, 2004, p 309). It is important to note that being a woman in itself does not lead to vulnerability but instead it is the 'unequal, gendered power relations which limit women's access to and control over resources' (Bradshaw and Fordham, 2013, p 19).

Regardless of an individual's age, gender or circumstance, many people who have been affected by a disaster display an array of emotions including severe grief, shock, disorientation, denial, depression, sadness, guilt, anxiety and anger (Yanay and Benjamin, 2005).

Why do we need a book about social work in disasters?

It is commonly accepted that disasters on a global level will increase in frequency, range and number (Alston et al, 2019). Due to this increase, disasters are becoming an increasingly important aspect of social work theory, education and practice (Dominelli and Ioakimidis, 2015).

Social work is centred on supporting people, often the most vulnerable in society, and so practitioners can take on diverse roles in preparing for and responding to disasters. This places the social work profession in a unique position to represent the voices of disadvantaged and sometimes silenced groups. Social workers play an integral key worker role in disaster responses. Their skills, knowledge and expertise are essential requisites in an emergency. Their professional responsibilities and expertise include supporting survivors, the bereaved and those directly and indirectly affected by an emergency. Social workers are central to the key stages of disaster management and support: prevention, immediate relief and recovery and reconstruction. Disasters do not only impact on those directly affected but also individuals, families, groups and communities locally, nationally and internationally.

There is a scarcity of UK or England specific literature devoted to social work in disasters. Although the UK is not considered to be 'disaster prone' as compared to the Global South, as this book will demonstrate, it has experienced a number of devastating disasters (Cleary and Dominelli, 2020). To our knowledge this is the first book to be published focusing upon the role of social workers in disasters from an England perspective. This book will outline the unique position that social workers occupy in disasters, and offers a voice to personal and professional experiences. We intend to emphasise the often overlooked and vital role that social workers play in disasters and to provide the reader with a context to understand the diversity of the roles undertaken by social workers and the significance of these roles in relation to responding to disasters.

It is important to share and develop knowledge, skills, best practice and learning from disasters nationally and internationally from the social workers who have been directly involved in emergency responses as well as from the communities they have served.

Equality, diversity and inclusion

Our aim is for this book to be as inclusive as possible and for authentic voices from those with lived personal and professional experience of disasters to be amplified. Every experience is unique, yet there are parallels that can be drawn from some of the contributions within the chapters. In this book, we hope to carefully balance validating the experiences of *all* individuals affected by disasters while recognising the broader picture which shows that individuals and communities already marginalised are further impacted by disasters.

Therefore, we invite you to read this book through the lens of intersectionality. Intersectionality is a concept introduced by Kimberlé Crenshaw over 30 years ago; speaking more recently, she described it as '*a lens, a prism, for seeing the way in which various forms of inequality often operate together and exacerbate each other*' (in Steinmetz, 2020). An intersectional approach is rooted in an understanding of the lived experiences of those who face multiple forms of oppression – for example, relating to their gender identity, race, class, sexuality, disability, age, immigration status and religion – and how these experiences intersect and create distinct experiences. As social workers we seek to understand the complexity of people's experiences and identities that can act as barriers in terms of how they access support and how professions, the media and society relate to them. We explore some of these important issues implicitly and explicitly in some of the following chapters and invite you to read this book with this intersectional lens. Whenever you see the following symbol ✹ in this book, this will act as a prompt to view each section through an intersectional lens.

Social context

Because nothing remains static, major worldwide events have occurred during the writing of this book, the most obvious being the Covid-19 global pandemic which has irreversibly changed our professional and personal lives and the fabric of society and will be further explored in Chapter 5. In the midst of global lockdowns, national restrictions, the death toll rising, people gasping for breath in overcrowded hospitals, debates about the safety of vaccines, as we wore masks to protect others and used sanitiser to protect ourselves, life somehow continued. From the public inquiries and inquests into historical disasters to new ones emerging, disasters occur within a social as well as a geographical context and we cannot and should not ignore other tragedies and major events that have occurred in the past two years. These include an earthquake in Haiti, extreme heatwaves, droughts, wildfires and flooding, the withdrawal of US troops in Afghanistan and the humanitarian crisis that is currently unfolding with fears for women and children in particular. However, we will highlight two tragic murders that took place during the writing of this book – that of George Floyd in the USA and the murder of Sarah Everard in England. Both murders resonate in relation to racism and women's rights – which are fundamental to the values of the social work profession.

On 25 May 2020, George Floyd, a 46-year-old Black man, was murdered by Derek Chauvin, a white police officer in Minneapolis, USA. Footage of the arrest showed the police officer kneeling on Floyd's neck while he was pinned to the floor. Floyd can be heard saying more than 20 times during the restraint that he could not breathe. In the middle of a global pandemic, and despite much of the world living in regional lockdowns, the strength of feeling of injustice was such that the death of George Floyd sparked protest marches across the world. Many of the protesters marched as part of the Black Lives Matter movement which campaigns for justice, equality and an end to racism. Floyd's murder sparked the largest racial justice protest in the USA since the Civil Rights movement and rippled across the world. The murder of George Floyd is one of many 'atrocities and brutalities endured by the global Black community' (Reid, 2020). The impact of the brutal murder of George Floyd and the subsequent resurgence of the global Black Lives Matter movement highlight the overt racism but also the cumulative effects of microaggressions that our Black, Asian and majority ethnic friends, colleagues and service users experience relentlessly on a daily basis. These microaggressions are interwoven in words, actions and social injustices which, whether intentional or not, are always hurtful and damaging.

Less than a year later, in March 2021, Sarah Everard went missing in London as she walked home from a friend's house, triggering a major police investigation. Her body was found in woodland in Kent a week after her disappearance. A London Metropolitan police officer, Wayne Couzens, was convicted of her kidnap, rape and murder. The abduction and murder of Sarah Everard precipitated a national protest, encouraging women to share their experience of feeling unsafe walking on the streets, sexism and sexual assault with several demonstrations taking place across the UK. At the time of Sarah Everard's murder, an online campaign, Everyone's Invited, was set up inviting people to post anonymous testimonies of sexual assault and harassment. This prompted more than 8,000 testimonies from girls as young as nine years of age – with numerous schools facing allegations of rape culture (BBC, 2021a).

The murders of George Floyd and Sarah Everard – as well as others, such as Nicole Smallman and Bibaa Henry – demonstrate that a systematic change is necessary to achieve a more egalitarian society that acknowledges the impact of historical inequalities. Anti-discriminatory practice is a fundamental tenant of the social work profession, yet it operates within structurally oppressive, sexist and racist systems, policies, politics and organisations. As a profession we play a fundamental role in reshaping these systems to ensure that every human right is promoted and valued. Many of the disasters around the world, be they in London, Haiti or Afghanistan, have caused immeasurable pain and suffering to many but in particular to marginalised groups who have the greatest need of help.

Self-care

Disasters are highly emotional and life-changing events; the emotions entangled within them linger with us and for some they never go away. In the final chapter we will explore in more detail the impact of disaster work and trauma-informed practice. It has been important to us as editors to ensure that the voices of those with lived experience within this book are centre stage. To this end, we have worked closely with each contributor who has told us their story and checked with them at each stage that we have captured it accurately and authentically. Their words are powerful, thought-provoking, and necessary for us to hear. Some readers may find some content distressing and so we advise that you take all the time you need when reading, with regular breaks in between, and reach out for support if needed. We will remind you of the need for self-care at the beginning of each chapter.

The role of the British Association of Social Workers (BASW)

Since 2017 BASW England has been working to raise awareness and to formalise the important role that social workers play in disaster recovery. Events in 2017 including the Grenfell fire, the Manchester Arena bombing and the attacks on Westminster Bridge and London Bridge made the need to articulate the role of social workers in disasters all the more urgent. Response to these tragic events demonstrated some creative social work practice, yet they also exposed a lack of systematic preparedness and training for social workers called upon to support individuals and their communities in these instances.

The BASW England Social Work in Disasters Working Group was formed to seek clarity and support the role of social workers in disasters. The Working Group has brought together academics, social work leaders, social work practitioners with experience of working in disasters, people impacted by disasters and other professionals with expertise in this area of work to share experiences and knowledge. One of the key achievements of the Working Group has been the development of the statement on the role of the Directors of Adult Social Services (DASS) and social workers in disaster recovery.

Another key achievement of the Working Group has been to develop a national continuous professional development (CPD) *Guidance on Social Work Roles Undertaken during Disasters*. This has been achieved by utilising the expertise of the Working Group and the knowledge shared by social workers and those who have experienced and been impacted by disasters. The guidance also integrates existing research and evidence in this area of work. The CPD guidance covers three core areas:

1. Knowledge and understanding.

2. Evaluation and analysis.

3. Skills and application.

Aspects of practice that are highlighted include the importance of self-care, prioritising the perspectives of those who have been affected or impacted by disasters while also reflecting upon the wider contexts, causes and implications of disasters. The guidance is mapped against the Professional Capabilities Framework and the Knowledge and Skills Statements. It is envisaged that this guidance will contribute to the initial steps towards a nationally co-ordinated and consistent approach to the training and development of disaster-informed social workers. Some ideas for how this ongoing role can be established are also shared in this guidance, including the potential for creating a register of disaster-informed social workers.

Given the life-changing and dramatic impact that disasters have on people's lives, the question of ethical practice is often at the fore and so links will be made to BASW and the International Federation of Social Work (IFSW) Codes of Ethics.

BASW England has organised several events to bring together social workers and individuals who have been impacted by disasters to share their experiences. This has included conferences and symposiums held in Durham, Manchester and Birmingham. The poignant stories shared at these events have highlighted examples of exceptional practice but also areas for further development. What became apparent during these conferences is that disasters, as they happen, attract a significant amount of attention. The generosity of the general public and professionals is evident. However, in the months and years following the disaster, there is often no space for people to share their feelings or experiences – this book serves to address this gap. This book will focus on the poignant and important personal stories of people with lived experiences of disaster. This will also include voices of social workers and their organisational leaders who have been directly involved in providing support in disasters, their reflections as well as sharing learning for the future. This book is particularly relevant in the context of an ever-changing unpredictable global and national environment, where disaster can strike at any time. It is hoped that the messages from the book can be applied to various forms of disasters.

How this book is structured

Maintaining the authentic voice of social workers and those impacted by disaster has been an important aspect of putting this book together. Chapter contributors include those with lived experiences, practitioners and social work leaders and academics. At the beginning of each chapter, we will remind you of the importance of self-care and at the end of each chapter we will offer some reflective questions for your consideration and suggestions for further reading.

In the following chapters you may notice that contributors recall the same incident differently. Each perspective is valid and while the general outline of a memory might be similar, the version of events will be impacted by individual experiences and the emotions entangled with the event. Memories are flexible and can be influenced by several factors. You might notice a change in emphasis as each contributor shares their story from their unique standpoint, adding authenticity.

Chapter 2: The invisible profession: social work during the 2020 health pandemic

This chapter is written by Professor Lena Dominelli. Lena has specific interests in projects on climate change and extreme weather events. She has created green social work as a new paradigm for theory and practice. She has conducted research in disaster work and published widely in social work, social policy and sociology. Lena currently chairs the International Association of Schools of Social Work (IASSW) Committee on Disaster Interventions, Climate Change and Sustainability and is involved in BASW's work in social work in disasters.

In this chapter, Lena considers the invisibility of social work during disasters, and the need to bring it into greater public focus. Covid-19 will then be reflected upon as an example of a disaster that provides many lessons for enhancing the visibility of the profession.

Chapter 3: My story: people with lived experience

This chapter is written from the perspective of people with lived experience within the context of disasters, including Hillsborough, Covid-19 and the Grenfell Tower fire. The contributors are as follows.

Margaret Aspinall

Margaret is the chair of the Hillsborough Family Support Group, whose son, James, an avid Liverpool football supporter, at the age of 18, was one of the 97 people who were unlawfully killed in the semi-final match between Liverpool and Nottingham Forest on 15 April 1989. Together with others, Margaret has fought tirelessly for over 30 years for truth and justice surrounding what has become known as the Hillsborough disaster. She tells her story of social work involvement in her life following James' death.

Reshma Patel

Reshma is an expert by experience consultant at Birmingham City University who lives with arthrogryposis – a lifelong condition. Reshma shares personal diary extracts which outline the emotional and practical challenges she faced living through the pandemic with an underlying health condition.

Zoë Dainton and Edward Daffarn

Zoë Dainton and Edward Daffarn are members of the Grenfell United Committee. Edward is a registered social worker who previously worked in community mental health, and Zoë is, at the time of writing, about to begin her first role as a newly qualified social worker in a community mental health team. Both share their personal and deeply moving recollections of the fire, reflecting on how it impacted every sphere of their lives. Given their professional ties to social work, both also reflect on the social work response to the disaster.

Chapter 4: My voice – experiences of social workers

This chapter gives a voice to social work practitioners, who are often overlooked during and after a disaster. The disasters referred to include the Manchester Arena bombing, Kegworth air disaster, Hillsborough disaster, Covid-19 and Grenfell fire. The contributors are as follows.

Elizabeth Stevens

Elizabeth is a social work manager who was called out to respond to the 2017 Manchester Arena bombing. Within her raw, honest extract, she reflects on how the disaster impacted on her both personally and professionally, and how it has influenced her practice forever.

Janet Foulds

Janet, a social work manager with over 30 years' experience in the sector, is the second contributor. Janet was involved in the response to both the Kegworth air crash (1989) and the Hillsborough disaster. Within this section, she reflects on the varied organisational/structural responses to each disaster including practical and emotional support, the importance of collaborative working, and the impact on her personal and professional life.

Professor Lucy Easthope

Lucy is a leading authority on recovering from disaster, and an advisor to the Prime Minister's Office following the Grenfell Tower fire on 14 June 2017. She is a co-founder of the After Disaster Network, University of Durham, which was set up to examine learning from these major tragedies. In her extract, Lucy reflects on her personal and professional response to the disaster, advises on how best to support practitioners, and discusses what she learned from both frontline social workers and survivors about best practice in disaster contexts.

Emma Bint

Emma is a social worker in Children's Services who provided support to families during the Covid-19 pandemic.

Joanne Bush

Joanne is an advanced practitioner who shares how her team adapted to the Covid-19 crisis in the early stages of the pandemic.

Chapter 5: Who will clap for us? The role of social workers during the Covid-19 pandemic

This chapter will focus on social work practitioners' experiences of working within the Covid-19 pandemic. In the midst of the most severe global pandemic for decades, social workers found themselves working in unfamiliar ways in extraordinary times. The Coronavirus Act 2020 went through Parliament in less than a week, suspending a range of previous legislation developed over years to support vulnerable children and adults (Legislation. gov.uk, 2020a). While this legislation is exceptional and temporary it has had a significant impact on the way that social workers practise within a legislative framework. This chapter will draw upon BASW's extensive survey with social workers during the Covid-19 pandemic to consider the experiences of practitioners working in various settings, their challenges and their messages.

A contribution will be made by a hospital social worker, practice educator and teacher, who writes about both the challenges faced and what is needed to ameliorate them, in the context of their practice during a global pandemic. Their contribution will remain anonymous and discusses how best to uphold social work values and ethics, which are often tested to the limit during disasters, coupled with the challenge of conflicting moral dilemmas.

Chapter 6: Learning for the future

In the final chapter, as editors we will draw together learning from the rich stories of those with lived experience, practitioners and their leaders. The role of trauma-informed practice and post-traumatic stress disorder for those who have witnessed and lived through a disaster will be explored. Sarah Dowd, the professional and safeguarding lead social worker at Princess Alice Hospice, will contribute to this chapter, sharing her experiences of making human connections in palliative care during a global pandemic. The impact of Covid-19 on the social work profession will be considered, and how disasters are never a one-off event; the impact is ongoing for individuals, families and communities. The legacy of disasters, in terms of how practice has changed, will be explored, together with the changing role of the media. The book will conclude with considering what the future might look like for social workers involved in disasters and how the BASW CPD guidance will be promoted as a recommended educational component in the preparation for disaster work.

Reflective questions

- Upon reading this chapter, how has your understanding of the definition of a disaster changed?

- Some people suggest that we never recover from a disaster, we just learn to live with the unacceptable. What are your thoughts on this?

Taking it further

Alston, M, Hazeleger, T and Hargreaves, D (2019) *Social Work and Disasters: A Handbook for Practice.* Oxon: Routledge.

BASW (nd) *CPD Guidance on Social Work Roles Undertaken during Disasters.* [online] Available at: www.basw.co.uk/system/files/resources/181086%20 CPD%20guidance%20on%20disaster%20social%20work%20V2.pdf (accessed 11 January 2022).

IFCR (nd) What Is a Disaster? [online] Available at: www.ifrc.org/what-disaster (accessed 11 January 2022).

CHAPTER 2

THE INVISIBLE PROFESSION: SOCIAL WORK DURING THE 2020 HEALTH PANDEMIC

Professor Lena Dominelli

Introduction

Social workers have been involved in assisting victim-survivors of disasters since they acquired professional status over a century ago. At times, they have also been victim-survivors themselves. Nonetheless they are expected to deliver a professional service. They offer practical aid including water, food, shelter, medicine, family reunification measures and psychosocial support. They remain long after the cameras have gone. However, they rarely appear before the cameras. In this brief chapter, I consider the invisibility of social work during disasters and my attempts to bring it into greater public focus. I then turn to Covid-19 as an example of a disaster that provides many lessons for enhancing the visibility of the profession globally.

Self-care

Some readers may find some content distressing. We advise that you take all the time you need when reading, with regular breaks, and reach out for support if needed.

Addressing the invisibility of social work

I became involved in disaster interventions when I watched the horrors of the 2004 Indian Ocean tsunami unfold on the television and not a social worker was in sight. All the other professions with an emergency remit were there talking about their work, but not social work. Why? My reaction as a doer was to initiate the Rebuilding People's Lives After Disaster Network (RIPL) and convince the Board of the International Association of Schools of Social Work (IASSW) to provide assistance locally. RIPL involved several IASSW member universities in supporting Sri Lanka in activities ranging from debris clearing to capacity building in social work. I had to climb a steep learning curve to help. Consequently, disasters became an issue that I wanted social work to take seriously. Over time, this included developing theory, practice interventions and curriculum development. It was tough figuring out how to do it, but combining practice and research, my endeavours grew incrementally.

In 2009, colleagues from Denmark and I organised the first international social work side-event at a United Nations Framework Convention on Climate Change, Conference of the Parties (UNFCCC COP) meeting in Copenhagen to raise awareness of social workers' roles in climate change disasters including supporting people fleeing from armed conflicts over water resources. I then wrote policy documents and initiated the Committee on Disaster Interventions, beginning with climate change for the IASSW Board. I amassed information on disasters of various kinds through research projects at Durham University where I was a co-director of the Institute of Hazard, Risk and Resilience (IHRR). One project dealt with climate change and older people in England. We constituted an interdisciplinary team led by a geographer with excellent leadership skills. This fostered my interest in extreme wea-ther events including floods, droughts and wildfires, and how social workers could become integrated into emergency teams. While at IHRR, I began volunteering to support victim-survivors in international disasters of diverse types to acquire practical experience.

In 2010, with the support of the then president of IASSW, I wrote an appli-cation for IASSW to be recognised as an observer to the UNFCCC among the research and independent non-governmental organisations (RINGOs) con-stituency. This was successful and I became IASSW's delegate representing social work at the subsequent COP meetings. I also organised side-events at several of them, including at COP21 in Paris in 2015. This raised social work's profile in disasters among French colleagues. Meanwhile, my interest in disasters deepened. I proceeded to undertake further research and support people in the field, including practitioner training. Within a decade, I had gone to many disaster spots, read on disasters extensively, and undertaken research headed by seismologists and geologists on earthquakes (Haiti, Wenchuan, Christchurch, Nepal), a complex disaster (Fukushima), hurricane (Haiyan), wild fires (Western Canada), floods (UK, Balkans) and extreme weather events (UK, Canada). Later, I worked with earth scientists on volcanoes and masks for use during ash fall. Some of my experiences led me to question the use of resources to take experts to stricken areas and consider the use of remote technologies to support victim-survivors. Following the Christchurch earthquakes, I developed the Virtual Helpline for Disasters which used Skype and email to support victim-survivors. It came into its own during the 2015 Gorkha earthquake in Nepal (Dominelli, 2018).

Working in such diverse disaster circumstances encouraged me to focus on transdisciplinary approaches to disasters. Working with physical scientists exposed me to their knowledge, while my sociological background highlighted for them the relevance of the social components of disasters. The social worker in me wanted to constantly critique and reflect upon the often top-down approaches to disasters, which I often felt wasted resources and excluded the very people that needed help. Lack of co-ordination among non-governmental organisations (NGOs) in a disaster arena produced erratic duplication of resources, eg, calls for children's books yielding endless copies of one and none of crucial others. Lack of control over NGO activities on the ground provided scope for predators to infiltrate vulnerable groups, eg, children in Sri Lanka and Haiti. Engaging with more experienced humanitarian aid workers, few of whom admitted to doing social work, made me realise the wide-ranging roles social workers adopted in disaster situations and argue for making visible their substantial contributions to disasters throughout the disaster cycle (Dominelli, 2011)

Many of my reflections on practice were endorsed by literature which was critical of disaster interventions, and I learnt of the disaster industrial complex that manufactured more misery for desperate, destitute people who struggled against the odds to carry on living in dignity (Klein, 2008; Szistova and Pyles, 2018). In contrast, my experience focused on local engagement and co-production in community-based solutions, bringing residents together with resource holders, teaching participatory action-research to enable residents to collect robust data to support their arguments with powerful others, and support bottom-up interventions. Realpolitik in some situations, eg, China, made me realise that only top-down-bottom-up approaches that created iterative loops between communities and those in charge would work. I also became aware of the importance of psychosocial interventions, not at the beginning of the disaster intervention cycle, but later when victim-survivors had integrated the enormity of their losses and grief within a new life built as they relinquished previous worries into the mists of time and memory. I also learnt how crucial it was for interventions to be locality-specific and culturally relevant, eg, local rituals, dance and food sharing to celebrate life without forgetting the dead.

This accumulated experience enabled me to acquire the confidence to write from a critical reflective perspective and address an issue that worried me greatly about social work approaches to disasters espousing an ecological and environmental orientation. This was their conceptual failure to engage with the socio-economic and political macro-contexts in which disasters occurred. As I sought to theorise a way of dealing with this conundrum, I came up with green social work (Dominelli, 2012). Central to my critique was the argument that social workers' concern with social justice should not ignore the environmental injustice which went hand-in-glove with structurally induced social injustice, marginality and precarity.

Green social work (GSW) has now produced a new disaster paradigm for the profession. It locates disasters in their social dimensions and works with community residents to find alternative solutions to conventional responses. It argues that social development should be green to be sustainable and that humanity has a responsibility to care for planet earth to inhibit the loss of biodiversity and ensure long-term sustainability. GSW also worries about the lack of habitable infrastructures for marginalised, socially excluded people, eg, over a billion slum dwellers living without adequate access to clean water, electricity, transportation, communication, health and educational resources. In daily practice, this can mean advocating for decent housing, properly paid employment and social protection to overcome the confinement of the most susceptible people on the planet to poor-quality housing, low pay and ill health. It also means holding corporations accountable for restoring degraded environments. GSW advocates caring for the environment and using it sustainably. The knowledge and skills integral to GSW enable the profession to take its place at the disaster response table and engage with other responders with evidence-based confidence.

My limited engagement with the horrendous 2017 Grenfell fire in London made me realise that it was time for me to focus on the UK and its lack of preparation and training on disasters for social workers and convinced me that the social work curriculum had to cover disasters. Discussing this with the chief social worker for adult care after Grenfell prompted the formation of the England RoundTable on Social Work in Disasters under the auspices of the British Association of Social Workers (BASW), England. Along with various other colleagues, I have been involved in devising the *CPD Guidance on Social Work Roles Undertaken during Disasters* which has received ADASS (Directors of Adult Social Services) support. I have also worked with BASW England staff and colleagues to organise and present in seminars and webinars, and develop e-materials and recently a systematic literature review as a key resource for disaster work.

Finally, these activities culminated in the exciting development of the MSc in Disaster Interventions and Humanitarian Aid and two continuing professional development (CPD) workshop-based modules (The Social Dimensions of Disasters and Disaster Interventions from a Green Social Work Perspective) at the University of Stirling, Scotland due to begin in the 2021–22 academic year. These are firsts for social work in the UK.

Covid-19: an opportunity to reframe social work's roles in disasters

Covid-19 was recognised as an unusual disease like SARS in a medical caseload in Wuhan, China in December 2019. Li Wenliang, an ophthalmologist at Wuhan Central Hospital, conscientiously documented these cases of '*unusual pneumonia*' and reported his findings to the local medical authorities. His work was initially discredited, but as the coronavirus, SARS-Cov-2, became embedded in the city, the Chinese authorities reacted with a rapidity that took many by surprise, and later admitted their deficiencies in recognising the novel coronavirus. Li died of the disease on 7 February 2020. Having captured the nation's heart, he was posthumously declared a martyr, the highest honour given to Chinese citizens. Since then, the disease has spread to other countries and was declared a pandemic by the World Health Organization (WHO) on 11 March 2020. The numbers affected since then have risen dramatically.

By 11 May 2021, Worldometers (nd) reported 169,238,079 confirmed cases globally and 3,328,843 deaths. Confirmed cases and deaths varied according to country and responses. The USA topped the list with 33,542,128 confirmed cases and 596,836 deaths. Then came India with 23,340,456 cases and 254,225 deaths; Brazil with 15,282,705 cases and 425,540 deaths; France replaced Russia in fourth place with 5,800,170 cases and 106,935 deaths; and Turkey overtook Spain as number five with 4,123,230 cases and 43,589 deaths.

The professionals on the front line included doctors, health professionals, social workers, social care workers, carers, porters, cleaners, bus drivers and others who staff essential services, with many becoming infected and some losing their lives in the process. Among professionals who performed their caring duties, disproportionate numbers of those dying of Covid-19 were of Black, Asian and minority ethnic group heritages. The public lauded the brave efforts undertaken by doctors and health professionals in many countries. In the UK, a ritual, countrywide handclap for NHS workers took place every Thursday evening at 8pm for ten weeks. But other professionals were rarely remarked upon. Thus, even when performing essential work under this health pandemic, the contributions of social workers and social care workers remained invisible. Thus, it is crucial that the profession tells their stories of heroism, hardship, angst and sacrifice during this pandemic. Their stories deserve to be told. I contribute to the telling of these narratives by drawing upon my experiences of supporting social workers who contacted me remotely through the Virtual Helpline, Skype, Zoom, Teams and the old reliable email forms as Covid-19 raged across the world.

Covid-19 catches the profession unprepared

The Covid-19 health pandemic caught everyone unawares, and consequently social workers were badly prepared for the realities that eventually confronted them, especially the structural inequalities exposed by the coronavirus. Every country was different in its socio-economic and political orientation, but social workers often faced the same problems: inadequate personal protective equipment (PPE); insufficient numbers of social care beds and hospital beds to ensure that each individual that needed one could access the necessary services without endangering others; insufficient community-based resources; willing but poorly trained volunteers and not enough staff to support and supervise them properly; and insufficient technological capacity and hardware among both social workers and service users in disadvantaged areas and those poorly served by broadband and internet providers. Many social workers also highlighted the lack of disaster training, a view evidenced by 100 questionnaires returned by participants in two short courses I offered on disasters – one in Durham in 2018 and one in Stirling in 2019.

Social work responses to Covid-19 bring out the best in the profession

In typical social work fashion, practitioners responded to the crisis unfolding before them with dedication and commitment, and seeking resources by reaching out to others. I was fortunate enough to be one of those they reached out to, and I am sure I learned more from them than they did from me. However, they certainly prompted me to make use of the excellent physical science training I had received as an undergraduate. The social workers from Wuhan wanted to know about the virus, masks, disinfectants and much else, so I read *The Lancet*, *Nature*, other scientific journals not usually accessed by social workers, and materials from the WHO website. I translated their dense scientific language into easy-to-use English which social workers then translated into Chinese. From my Chinese colleagues, I learnt about the amazing range of activities that social workers performed. I was able to reflect upon and subsequently use these lessons in other countries as Covid-19 turned into a global pandemic affecting every country on earth.

These included roles that I found challenging: disinfecting streets and public places, taking temperatures of residents going about their business to ensure that those who were ill returned home. Social workers also performed the tasks normally associated with their work – providing food, medicines, taking sick people to hospital, providing services to marginalised groups, particularly older people and disabled persons, crisis interventions, and public health education or consciousness raising about Covid-19 including the importance of residents adhering to wearing masks, washing hands often with soap and water or hand sanitisers, disinfectant wipes and social distancing. When matters went awry, they were filled with grief, eg, when they discovered that a disabled child had been left alone for a while when both parents were hospitalised to receive medical care for Covid-19. Their community social work was impressive as they worked the large neighbourhoods to which local officials had assigned them with care, thoroughness and dignity, giving service users person-centred practice and respect. These social workers were also inventive. They devised services when they saw a gap, using technology to bring people and resources together, eg, the Community Online and Offline Interdisciplinary and Interprofessional Model in Shaanxi Province.

Their motto of 'serve the people' motivated them to incredible heights. And, like their Western counterparts, they remained largely unsung heroes. Not that they ask for or expect praise for doing the work they love. Like many practitioners in the West, those who also held positions in academia found they had to teach classes online and learn how to assess practice skills in various ways. Another commonality in both China and the West was people's willingness to help whenever they could, even if it meant exposing themselves to the coronavirus with inadequate PPE. Chinese and Western social workers made use of peer support groups to check out difficult cases, consider what they should do and offer constructive help and support to each other to get through their workloads to deliver the best possible services to those in need. Social work practice at its best is excellent, even under stressful, under-resourced circumstances when practitioners often felt left to 'get on with it' without much managerial support. Their work was often inspirational, eg, in India where government policies ignored millions of migrant workers who lost their jobs and were left without resources to trek thousands of kilometres unaided. Social work academics, practitioners and students created self-help resources for them through collective endeavours which involved individuals giving money to support these endeavours. Managers were often overworked, understaffed and inadequately supervised. But the uncertainty of fighting an unknown assailant brought different groups together to help one another provide needed services and survive themselves from day-to-day. Seeking managers as allies is an important aspect of top-down-bottom-up approaches to Covid-19. They are often isolated and squeezed by being caught between their superiors higher in the labour hierarchy and the practitioners they supervise.

There were also important differences between countries. The movement of people, many of whom were unknowingly carrying the coronavirus but showing no symptoms, caused many problems for social workers who were not backed up with 'test, track and trace' facilities to control the virus effectively. In India, social workers, academic staff and students were impressive in organising to feed the millions without food, shelter or other resources. Many, as did their counterparts in the West, dug into their own pockets to feed those in need. In one place in South Africa, the queues for food parcels stretched for several kilometres, highlighting the need for considerable resources to be placed at the disposal of social workers. Others became good fundraisers using social capital and social networks to bring people together, pool resources and meet need. In Ethiopia, social work academics and students in universities took the lead in organising self-help initiatives based on district level networks to provide food for marginalised groups who had none. While Covid-19 has decimated populations globally, especially among the elderly through community-based transmission, social work has lived up to its value base of helping those in need, providing services while respecting people and their wishes, offering solidarity and co-ordinating people and resources to alleviate suffering and hardship. These are also the anti-oppressive values that we need to rebuild the post-Covid-19 world. Add to these caring for the environment in daily practice, eg, improving housing infrastructures and access to medical care and social resources for homeless service users, and you include a key tenet of GSW.

In other countries, earlier disasters had made social workers better prepared to meet the demands of the pandemic. People had practised their emergency drills and collected their resources to survive without help for a while, eg, Taiwan, which immediately demanded that travellers from China quarantine at its borders to control the spread of the coronavirus among the broader populace. However, this assailant was different. People could not see 'the enemy', they only knew it had invaded their body when they became ill. While many had the advantages of preparedness, not being phased in an emergency, this pandemic questioned their ontological position and challenged their certainties. For some, this caused mental anguish and emotional distress.

This was not an easy issue for them to discuss with others. In some countries, eg, Zimbabwe, mental health issues are taboo, and seldom admitted because doing so would attract shame and stigma for the family.

Other practitioners in countries like Slovenia, Australia and the UK were tormented by the thought of not being able to determine whether service users were experiencing heightened levels of abuse – physical, sexual, financial and domestic abuse – but not receiving the support they required. These social workers often felt disempowered by not knowing whether they needed to intervene. Others were perturbed that social isolation and the inadequate housing that people were being confined to during long periods of lockdown might produce mental ill health that might not be diagnosed and addressed without face-to-face home visits, which were often discouraged. Some social workers experienced ethical dilemmas when risk assessments suggested that home visits were unnecessary, or PPE was unavailable, because depriving people of needed services undermined their professional ethics and commitment. In the UK, social workers, supported by BASW, challenged those provisions of the Coronavirus Act 2020 that sought to suspend the duty to assess and meet unmet eligible needs under the Care Act 2014.

Taiwan succeeded in controlling the spread of the virus by enforcing quarantines on visitors from China from the beginning of the outbreak. There were requirements on social distancing, rationing of PPE, and not interacting with others. As in other countries, social workers had to ensure that people had sufficient food and medicines to maintain health and well-being. However, they worried that social isolation, especially among older people, would undermine their mental health. Social workers were responsible for track and trace endeavours alongside their normal workloads, and this created feelings of stress and overwork among significant numbers of them. Social workers also engaged in public awareness campaigns, explaining government policies to residents so that they could look after themselves as required during the pandemic. They also distributed funds to those financially affected by the pandemic, including businesses. And they could fine those who violated public health requirements. Lack of co-ordination between social workers, the police and village officials meant that individuals could be asked about the same issue by all of them. This frustrated many residents. Homeless people expressed hostility to social workers intervening in their lives, including suggestions regarding self-care. Social workers themselves were subjected to surveillance and had to have their temperatures checked before entering their offices. Surveillance in many countries, especially the USA, raised questions about human rights and what rights should be sacrificed for the greater good.

In South Korea, as in other countries, masks were in short supply at the beginning of the pandemic. Restricting travellers and robust track and trace systems quickly brought Covid-19 cases under control, although a significant cluster of infections among a religious group had the authorities worried for a while. Social workers relied heavily on NGOs to provide services to those affected by the disaster. Other Asian countries that had relative successes in controlling the coronavirus include Hong Kong, Singapore and Malaysia. Here, as in Taiwan and China, social workers played much wider roles than they did in the West. It is crucial that social workers share experiences and learn lessons from abroad. They have much to teach us.

Conclusion

Social workers across the world have responded to anticipated and new challenges during disasters. They perform a vast array of roles to protect people and provide services to victim-survivors. Their prime concern to serve and uphold human rights and social justice even in the most extreme conditions can result in their risking their own health and well-being to do so. However, their heroic endeavours remain unacknowledged in the public arena, where many are unaware of the essential work that they do. Getting such recognition requires engagement with the traditional and social media so that myths about social work are shattered. Achieving this goal requires collective action that can be facilitated by social work's professional associations. Social workers do more than safeguard children and adults, so much more! Additionally, their values of promoting human rights, social justice including environmental justice and serving others to show solidarity in meeting need, are those that will be invaluable in creating a brighter, more egalitarian future in the post-Covid world. Tackling climate change to obtain climate justice becomes another strand in that work. This provides an optimistic agenda for action together.

Reflective questions

- What do you think might be the reason that social workers, as a profession, remain invisible during disasters?
- How can social workers and other professionals learn with communities during a disaster?

Taking it further

Dominelli, L (2019) Green Social Work, Political Ecology and Environmental Justice. In Webb, S A (ed) *The Routledge Handbook of Critical Social Work* (pp 233–43). London: Routledge.

Dominelli, L (2021) A Green Social Work Perspective on Social Work during the Time of Covid-19. *International Journal of Social Welfare*, 30(1): 7–16.

CHAPTER 3

MY STORY: PEOPLE WITH LIVED EXPERIENCE

The voices of people with lived experience of disasters are often marginalised. Throughout every disaster in living memory, media and government departments (at both a local and national level) have dominated the discourse and framed narratives according to their own agenda. The voices of the bereaved and survivors are (in many cases intentionally) edited out of history.

This erasure not only privileges the accounts of those in power, widening the schism of inequality, but it also leads to a loss of valuable learning which could be used to prevent, or ameliorate the response to, future disasters.

This chapter is designed to provide social workers with the unique opportunity to truly listen to, and learn from, such voices – an opportunity which is rare, if it ever presents itself, for social workers of all levels and disciplines. It is designed to be a safe space through which people with lived experience are invited to speak their truth without fear, with their consent and in their control.

All of the stories you find below are written by those with lived experience in their own time and through the medium they felt would captures their voice best; for some, this meant putting pen to paper, and for others this meant telling their story with an editor who put pen to paper on their behalf, before developing the piece alongside them.

Each survivor's story is individual; however, commonalities between them include an overview of the disaster in their own words, a brief look at challenges faced and what, if any, were the helping factors. The stories also contain a reflection on the social work response, as well as key messages for social workers, managers and directors of all levels.

BASW England is deeply grateful to those who so bravely shared their stories in the hope that practitioners, and future survivors and family members, could benefit from their insight and experience. We hope each story can be used to reflect on, remember and honour those who are sadly no longer with us.

Our James

Margaret Aspinall

Margaret is the chair of the Hillsborough Family Support Group. Her son, James Aspinall, an avid Liverpool football supporter, at the age of 18, was one of the 97 people who died on 15 April 1989. Together with others, Margaret has fought tirelessly for over 30 years for truth and justice surrounding what has become known as the Hillsborough disaster. She tells her story of social work involvement in her life following James' death.

Hillsborough football disaster

On 15 April 1989, a Football Association (FA) Cup semi-final football match between Liverpool and Nottingham Forest was hosted at a neutral ground. The match was held in Hillsborough in Sheffield, a city in Yorkshire. The game was expected to draw more than 53,000 fans.

Liverpool fans were allocated the smaller end of the Hillsborough stadium, Leppings Lane, which had an entrance with a limited number of turnstiles. At the time, it was common practice in football grounds to have standing terraces divided into 'pens' by high fences that contained fans in blocks, separating them from the pitch. Due to a lack of system, fans were not evenly distributed among the pens, neither was there a system to count the number of people in each pen. The inadequate number of turnstiles outside Leppings Lane could not cope with the large crowd and the police decided to open an additional gate causing severe crushing in the already overcrowded pens.

Despite CCTV cameras showing horrific images of distress in the crowd to the Ground Control Room and to the Police Control Box, together with police presence on perimeter of the pitch, the immediate response has been heavily criticised for being unorganised and slow. Both the police and ambulance service at the scene failed to recognise the event as a major incident which caused tragic delays to people needing emergency care.

A total of 97 people died – and were unlawfully killed. Of these, 38 were children or teenagers; the youngest was ten years old. A further 766 people were injured, and hundreds of families left bereft. The Hillsborough football disaster remains the biggest tragedy in British sporting history.

James was such a gentle lad; he was very generous, very kind, especially to his siblings. They all looked up to him. I am sure people say this all the time about their loved ones, but I can genuinely say James was such a beautiful person. He had a lovely job at the shipping company, Albion House, and was a hard worker. He was an altar boy. He used to get top marks at his school in Knowsley. I was very proud of him. I will always remember that he saved up and bought a guitar for his dad's birthday. His dad was so moved – he treasures that guitar to this day.

I often think how fortunate myself and Jim (my husband) were to have had James, to have known James. I was very blessed that God chose me to be his Mum. He was my first born and I did not just love him, I adored him.

People would say you have got four other children, but that does not change anything.

The day our lives changed forever – 15 April 1989

It was James' first away game; I was always concerned about him going away from home. I never used to allow it. Three weeks after his 18th, he said, '*Ah mum, you can't stop me now, I'm 18 and I've got a ticket to the game.*' I do not know why it worried me really because Liverpool did not have any trouble at the grounds at that time.

That morning he got up and was all excited. As he left, he asked what time his nine-year-old sister Kerry would be home. She had been in Cornwall with her aunty for a week. He said, '*Keep her up until I'm home. I haven't seen her all week.*'

The last thing he said to me was '*I will go to mass in the morning.*' So, I said, '*Okay*'. I just watched him walk up the road. It was a very strange thing; I thought to myself then, God, isn't he lovely? I said to myself proudly '*That's my son.*' The first thing Kerry said when she got home was '*Where's our James?*' She was all excited.

That afternoon, Kerry's aunt turned on the TV. She said, '*There is trouble at Hillsborough.*' You could see people getting laid down on the pitch, fans carrying people. I said, '*Oh my god, have these people fainted?*'

I thought, '*I hope James is nowhere near there.*'

As fatalities began to be announced, I thought '*This can't be happening.*' Soon, an emergency number was issued. We kept phoning but could not get through. The kids were crying, and I was just telling them, in fact I was shouting at them, to be quiet. My husband phoned, and he said, '*Have you heard from James?*' I said '*No. Don't you dare come home without him.*' He went to the hospitals to see if he was on any lists.

In the meantime, I called the coach company, who said all passengers had been accounted for, and buses would return at midnight. The relief was unbelievable. At midnight, we went to Lime Street Station. We waited for every coach to come in. That is what gets me. We went to the police station and an officer said *'Go home Mrs Aspinall. As soon as the list comes through, we will get in touch.'* Jimmy went to Sheffield to find James. I stayed in case James returned, Jimmy agreed to ring me every half an hour. When he did not ring at 4am, I thought there was something wrong. At 6am, Kerry said *'You said James would be home. Where is he?'* I bawled *'Get back into bed.'*

I was walking to the top of the road and saw my brother-in-law and husband in the car without James. As they got out, I could see Jimmy had been sobbing. He just said *'Marg'*. I started to run, I had to get away. I said *'Don't catch me up. If you do not, my son is still alive.'* I carried on running. As I looked up, I saw my husband on the floor. I asked, *'Jim, it's true, is it?'* He replied that he was sorry. He held a clear bag with James' belt, watch, ID, and match ticket. I said, *'I don't want that, I just want James. Please do not give me them, give me James.'* I wanted to go to Sheffield then. I said, *'James will be feeling the cold, he's left his big coat.'*

I will always remember going into the room where he was. It was eerie and dark, with these curtains pulled across. A voice asked, *'Are you ready?'* and I thought *'Ready for what?'* When the curtains opened, I said *'I've got to put his coat on.'* He said *'No, he doesn't belong to you, it belongs to the coroner.'* I was livid telling them *'He does not belong to the coroner, he's mine. The umbilical cord has never been cut properly.'* Outside, all you could hear were families crying. I thought *'Why are they crying? They didn't know James.'* They were crying for their loved ones – I did not realise it at the time.

Aftermath and recovery

The effect on the younger children, who were only seven and nine, was devastating. And my older son, who was 16, not only lost his brother, he lost his best friend. He became the eldest. I remember having to go to hospital because it was thought I had cancer, I lost so much weight and went very thin – I was not eating. My daughter said, *'I don't want you to die, like my brother.'* That was a wake-up call. When I was a child, I lost a baby brother. My mum asked me *'Do you ever think about him?'* and I said, *'No. You never talk about him.'* She said, *'That was a mistake, I tried to hold the pain in – it nearly killed me. Don't do the same thing.'*

I have not recovered, none of us have. You can't recover from losing a child. You learn to live with it. With Hillsborough, Grenfell and other disasters there has been no accountability. You can never come to terms with the loss. There is still no justice. When I see my grandchildren, they bring me so much joy, but something is always missing. James never got to see them. But he did nothing wrong. He was in the ground early, had a ticket, had not drunk anything – so why is he dead?

The Hillsborough Families Support Group has helped through these difficult years – you can either be selfish and say, '*I'm not interested, my son's gone why should I care about anyone else?*' or support one another, like James would have wanted. My children, my husband, my family and the campaign have got me through this; without them I would have been suicidal.

My message to social workers: do not ever give up

The first time there was a knock on the door, and I heard the words 'social worker' I was angry. I thought why the hell are they here? I remember saying '*I have never done anything wrong to my children in my life.*' They tried to explain, '*We are not here for that Margaret, we are just here to see if you need any support.*' I replied, '*I've got family and friends. I do not need anyone else. Go away.*'

I can only say, thank God for Antoinette (the long-term social worker), for her persistence. She kept coming back, even after the insults. Once she visited on Christmas Day and took me to the cemetery. That is something that I call a wonderful service. Keep persisting. In the end friends go away and in the end your family go away. They get sick of looking at you upset and hearing about your grief. I can understand that. When my brother lost his daughter, I did not know what to say or do. I had been through it, but I still did not know how to handle our Ray. Getting that knock at the door is a shock for families. It is nicer to put a note or a letter through the letterbox with your name and contact number on it and explain who you are. Explain that you are not there to intrude on the grief.

Social workers need to listen to what people have to say and what they feel angry about, especially after injustice. Do not ever give up. My message to managers would be to provide disaster training. Social workers need to understand historical and current injustices. They must learn from families and let people tell their story.

I still get emotional when I talk about James because I can see his face now smiling at me.

My brother

Anon

> *For the purpose of this chapter the author will remain anonymous, and the names have been changed to respect the wishes of individuals involved. As highlighted in other chapters, people do not always have the opportunity to say goodbye to their loved ones in a disaster – there is no preparedness for the brutality of loss in such circumstances. The section ends rather abruptly – a decision made by the author which illustrates the unexpectedness of loss.*

My brother. My big, rugged bear of a brother is dead. Taken, no, killed by a virus. A silent deadly killer virus like we have never known before. One with the power to fracture lives, families, communities. The world. Creeping silently, stealthily treading its path from Hubei to Hanoi to Hanover, then a shire. Imperceptibly and then at warp speed.

Following in its wake the imposition of lockdown was like a domino effect. We observed the rules as soon as we caught up. Standing in the kitchen in shocked silence when Boris told us on Monday night that the virus is locking us up.

We looked at our surroundings. We're luckier than most. We have each other, and one out of four of our children with us in beautiful surroundings. Our nearest neighbours are 50 times the 'legal' minimum distance from us. We worried about Karen and the loss she was enduring. Wrenched back from uni too soon. All her plans shattered. *'No biggie in the scheme of things though'*, she said.

We worried for our elderly parents in poor health. The vulnerable, the elderly. We worried about spreading it to our elderly neighbour. *'It's worse than the war'*, she said, as we stopped on our bikes. You can't see the enemy. What you are contending with.

We worried about those less fortunate. The families in flats in tower blocks, with no money. We worried about the rise in domestic violence, the impact on mental health, the economy, our futures. We worried about society, the community. We clapped for our carers. We were bewildered by the scale of the change. We felt the sun shining on our faces for those first few days. It feels like the earth is smiling at us for giving it a break, we said. Surely there will be some permanent change to behaviour, we speculated.

We went through the cycle of loss many times a day. Sometimes many times an hour. Denial, anger, bargaining. Never quite reaching acceptance. We reached Friday night. We raised a glass to each other. *'We've survived the week'*, we cheered. We can manage this loss of liberty, this oppression, together. *'It's not even a week'*, we realised two sips in. Five days. *'We can do this'*, we said. *'We are more fortunate than most.'*

At the weekend we patted ourselves on the back for finding a new circular walk from the house. We sat on a bench surrounded by daffodils, where the words *In memory of x, the road not travelled* were inscribed. *'Sit there if you like, it's a lovely view'*, said the man we presumed to be her husband. So, on Sunday we did. We ate our sandwiches and planned our retirement as we marvelled at the beauty and felt the freedom.

Reality came closer. My mum called: *'Your 70-year-old uncle is on a ventilator in hospital. The one you stayed with when you left for London at 18. You know, who plays golf three times a week.'* We spoke to a friend who works in A&E health on the frontline. *'It's affecting 40-, 50-year-olds too you know'*, she said. They must have underlying health conditions, we thought.

We worried more about our other children. We wanted to hold them tight. We researched flights back from Malaysia. We need to bring Penny home. She'll be so isolated when the domino spreads to Kuala Lumpur. We worried for Sue, working all hours, travelling daily on the tube, given more responsibility than we thought legal for a 22-year-old. Sue who'd cried most days this month. No wonder. But at least the children are together in London now.

'You're having a beer on Sunday night?' my daughter asked with a judgmental edge. *'Yep,'* I said. *'Back to work tomorrow. I need to pretend a little longer. It's easier for me though. At least I have structure to distract me from the loss. Of freedom, of connection.'*

The next day, I started work at 7.30am, reading papers for my first call with a cup of tea. We were together when my brother rang at 9.20am. We looked at each other aghast. We knew. *'Answer it'*, she says. *He'll be ringing about my uncle*, I think. I took a deep breath and answered. It was Cath. *'Are you okay?'* I ask, mindlessly, knowing she can't possibly be. *'No'*, she said. *'I'm sorry to have to tell you that your brother is dead.'* Cath, my sister-in-law of 35 years, who I have known since school. I hear a gasp from Linda, my partner. Or was that me, making that noise?

Cath sounded so calm. I struggled to speak. *'What can we do?'* I asked. *'Please just tell your mum and sister for me'*, she said. *'Of course, I can do that'*, I said. But how? How the hell do I do that? We ring my sister, we debate, we pack. We debate. We pack. We ring my sister. We pack. I empty the contents of the fridge into a bag. Linda gently takes the bowl of leek sauce from my hand. *'Do we really need that?'* she asks.

We debate, we pack, we ring my sister. I empty the contents of the dry food cupboard into a bag.

'How many days are we going for?' Linda adds gently, taking the tins of mackerel from the cupboard. *'I'll drive'*, I say. *'I need to be distracted and busy.'* They both checked, but, I was sure. *'Whatever is best for you'*, they say. *'But know you might not be quite right.'* I told them I would be careful.

We drive. We ring my sister. *'I'll get a taxi to Mum's'*, she says. *'I'll tell her.'* We ring Julie. A GP, she'll know. We ask about risk and safety. Should we hug her? Should we touch her? Should we hold her in our collective grief? Should we be even asking these fucking questions? She's so calm, so helpful. *'Stop at Waitrose'*, she says. *'They have emergency supplies for NHS staff. I'm sure they'll find you some wipes.'*

I drive. My sister rings. She's told Mum. I'll put her on. Mum, sobbing and sobbing. Don't come. Don't come she says. I can't bear it. It's all too much. I can't put you at risk. I pulled over. *'We're coming'*, I say. *'Even if it's just to stand in your garden and wave to you. We can stay somewhere else.'*

I am destroyed. I can't drive. I get in the back with my daughter, her granddaughter, his niece. We look for hotels. Nothing. Airbnb? Nothing. *'We'll have to drive back tonight'*, I thought. *'Are we doing the right thing? I know, I can ask a friend.'* We asked if anyone had an annexe or an empty house. *'We have a house you can use*', said Jack, my childhood friend, without hesitation. '*We'll make up beds for you downstairs. In Exeter. Near your sister. But not near your mum.*' We were so grateful. '*Are you sure? We don't want to put anyone at risk,*' we said. '*I'm sure. We'd love to have you with us.*' But we know.

We ring my sister. We plan our entry. '*You go straight up to the upstairs bathroom and wash your hands*', we agree. Only one of us in the kitchen at once. '*Have you got cleaner we ask? We'll stop at Tesco. Does mum need anything?*' '*Yes, bleach and milk.*' We said we would see what we could do, but we couldn't promise.

The queue outside Tesco snaked around the shop. One in one out. We'd forgotten for a minute. You can't just pop in anymore. '*I'll ask for help*', said Linda – '*I'm sure we count as an emergency.*' '*If you can't get in. Don't worry. We'll manage,*' I said. Slowly the shop manager realises what's being asked of her. I'll take you round the shop she says. Marigolds, bleach, soap. What else do you need? Look we have toilet roll. Take some.

We shout to Mum through the door. Straight upstairs as planned to the bathroom. We change clothes. Wash our hands, our face. Slowly we descend. Scared to go in. To go near Mum. We walk in. My sister moves two metres away. I stand. I look. I can't speak. My eyes fill up.

Is this really happening?

Reshma Patel

Reshma Patel is an expert by experience consultant at Birmingham City University, who lives with arthrogryposis – a lifelong condition. As somebody living with underlying health conditions, the coronavirus pandemic has been a particularly difficult period. Below is a collection of diary extracts, poems, and reflections which outline Reshma's experience.

I was almost 5000 miles away from home when the coronavirus hit, visiting India with my family. It was a trip I had always dreamt of. Living with a long-term health condition, I thought – okay, I have hit 50, and I need to get my travel plans going, otherwise my health will take a downturn and I will never make it.

After hiding the news from me, in the final week of my stay, my family in England finally called to tell me how serious the pandemic was back home.

I started panicking – I rely on personal assistants to provide me with 24/7 care, so I had so many questions running through my mind. I worried about how I would manage if they became ill, how to get hold of PPE, and how to keep myself safe when they would be in such close contact.

But my worries were not just confined to myself – I also live with my elderly dad, who has heart issues, and his well-being was also a huge concern. I wondered if social services would come and take over. I even wondered if we would all be taken off somewhere. I was so worried that I could not sleep.

When I returned home, one of my personal assistants was hesitant to come round, as she was concerned that I might have caught the virus overseas. Without thinking, I said, *'I don't know what to say. How am I going to manage? I still need support even through this difficult time.'* We managed to come to a compromise once I arranged transportation for her, but it was so stressful to balance her needs as an individual with my own. It is not easy being a disabled employer at the best of times, let alone in a pandemic.

I remember thinking *'Is this really happening? Has the whole world just crashed around us all?'* I really was not sure how to feel. I wanted to just hide away behind Candy Crush and hidden object games. As the weeks passed by, my usual motto *'Wake up with a smile, go to sleep with a smile, and let the day take care of itself'* began to wear thin. I tried so hard to keep it together, but at times I simply lost the will to live. Being at home all the time meant that I had far too much time to think. And beyond my mental health, physically, my body was aching all over. With so much stress, I worried about whether I would snap at someone.

Getting my basic needs met seemed impossible at times. Even accessing something as basic as food was a nightmare. My sister was scared to drive to my home to drop off meals at first, because scaremongers were saying that the police would fine people for leaving home. I felt so isolated.

During such a difficult time, three things helped me to get through – *purpose, connection* and *practical support*.

In terms of *purpose*, I have always been passionate about my work as an expert by experience consultant at the University of Birmingham, which was a good distraction – although I sometimes wonder if it was in fact an avoidance technique. But while it was helpful, it also came with more worries and responsibilities as I tried to advocate on behalf of so many other people with lived experience. I work with many people who are on zero-hour contracts, so I was dealing with lots of people who had lost income and were now relying on benefits. Sometimes I did not know where my issues ended and where theirs began.

In terms of *connection*, seeing loved ones helped. For example, having nephews and nieces over to feed them with junk that they can only get at my house. Beyond family, accessing online counselling and cognitive behavioural therapy (CBT) gave me the space I needed to talk. The aim of the CBT was to help me to tune in with my emotions, which was different, as I don't usually analyse myself too deeply – I'm much more a practical person.

I also joined an online theatre group, which was a lifeline. The group consisted of about 50 women having a laugh on Zoom telling their stories. It was really creative, we learnt new things, new methods of expressing ourselves. It was so diverse; we had people from different ethnicities and with disabilities, people in residential homes. It was refreshing just to do something light-hearted... it was both personal and emotional.

In terms of *practical support*, simple things like having transport arranged for my personal assistants, which meant they were well looked-after, alleviated stress on my part. Technically, the meals I received as a shielding person should have helped – but no one bothered to ask whether or not I was a vegetarian or had dietary requirements. I cannot stress enough just how important getting the basics right is.

Social care involvement

The only contact I received from social care was a phone call. Their one question was 'have you got enough PPE?' – it wasn't a meaningful connection at all, it was just like they were doing their weekly call. I had already sorted myself out by the time they called, which included finding 24/7 cover for personal assistants who were off with Covid-19. Believe me, this was an enormous task, not only in terms of logistics, but also in terms of allowing strangers into my home. For the first time in my life, I had to agree to people turning up at the door without having ever met them. After experiencing a theft from a previous personal assistant, it still takes so much now to trust someone new.

If I were to give some lasting messages to social workers supporting disaster survivors in the future, they would be as follows.

1. Try to help people to find solutions.

2. Offer different options.

3. Try to remember to contact the person regularly, even just to check in emotionally.

4. Make a clear action plan alongside the person you are supporting and be sure to follow up on this.

When I reflect on previous experiences with social workers, the best experience I had was with a social worker who didn't dismiss the fact that I was quite capable of doing things for myself. But she also knew how to gently offer support should I need it. She said, '*I know you can do things for yourself, but if there is anything I can take off you, would that help?*'

When it comes to advising social work managers and organisations, my advice would be to have clear back-up plans – and to be honest about what someone may miss out on when falling back onto this. As a disabled person, it matters to me that people are transparent, so I know exactly what to expect. Once I know and understand the truth, it makes the next steps easier to bear.

How are you?

A poem by Reshma Patel

How are you? I'm fine. Am I really? I don't know.

I'm scared, I'm calm, I'm strong, I'm vulnerable.
What is vulnerable?

I'm positive. I'm alert, I'm mindful, I'm distracted.
I'm relaxed and watchful.

I'm lucky, blessed, privileged, loved, supported.

I work, I walk, I talk, I eat. I try not to drink.

Facebook, family, cakes, games bring joy, and complicated
physical contact.

I enjoy my small world, but yearn for its expansion.

$\longrightarrow$

I deny myself the thoughts of the bigger world.

The future world, the spontaneous world, the
unlocked world.

When will the world be a place of safety? When will that be?

How even will this new world look like?

Everyone is uncertain, waiting for instructions.

But instructions don't help if you're classed as vulnerable.

I can go out, but will I? My health and safety is
in my own hands.

My future a series of personal step by step decisions.

Risk assessed, managed with every action that I take.

Every interaction, every gate post I touch.
Every parcel delivered.

Every stranger approaching. Every thought of
gathering again.

So unanchored, undecisive and uncertain.

Distance, I focus on the here and now.

With no safety in numbers for the vulnerable,

no net to catch those around me that keep me safe,
no blanket to envelop me,

no pair of immaculately clean hands to help me to put
my safety first.

Can I really allow myself to look into the future?

I dream that we will pass through this uneven world

of the safe and shielded safe spaces, and we will
be redefined.

And then we will return to healthy spaces, life,
filled with hugs,

happiness, holidays, friends and futures, uncomplicated
chance meetings.

We will be healthy, happy and safe.

This will end one day.

They stood with us

Zoë Dainton

Zoë Dainton is a survivor of the Grenfell Tower fire, as well as a Grenfell United Committee member. At the time of writing, she was about to begin her first role as a newly qualified social worker in a community mental health team.

Grenfell Tower fire

On 14 June 2017, a fire broke out in the kitchen of a fourth-floor flat in a 23-storey tower block in North Kensington, West London. Within minutes the fire engulfed the exterior of the building. Seventy-two people died. Hundreds of people lost loved ones, friends, neighbours and homes. The fire has become known as one of Britain's worst modern disasters. In the days after the fire, Grenfell United was formed, which is a group of survivors and bereaved families working together for the community and campaigning for safe homes and justice. A public inquiry has been set up and is ongoing. In his first report, the author, Sir Martin Moore-Bick, concluded that the use of aluminium composite material (ACM) cladding panels on Grenfell Tower was the '*primary cause of the rapid spread of fire up, around and down the building*' (Moore-Bick, 2019, p 21).

Am I ever going to recover from this?

Am I ever going to be able to sleep with the light off?

Am I ever going to be able to enter a high rise building ever again?

These are just some of my ruminating thoughts in the aftermath of the fire.

In many ways, it all feels like yesterday, even though three and a half years have passed.

I was on the fourth floor when it all began – the fire started in my neighbour's flat. I believe we were the last people to escape from our floor, because initially, we didn't think it was a big deal. But then a neighbour called to tell us that we needed to leave the building. I knew then that we had to act fast. When we left, the fire was quite small and contained. But within eight to ten minutes, it spread so quickly that the disaster had already taken hold. It is an image that will never leave me.

There are many misconceptions from those who have not lived through it. Some people think, *'Oh, you just lost a house, your clothes, your trainers – you'll get them back.'* But many don't realise that it is more than being uprooted from what we knew. While some of us have escaped, we have not escaped fully intact. We may have been rehoused, but we witnessed people die. It wasn't just that we had to rebuild a home – we had to rebuild ourselves. For me, this has been a process of literally finding out who I am again.

Major challenges

On a personal level, the fire has impacted every single area of my life – everything you can think of. It has changed sleep, mood, appetite and relationships. It has even altered my attitude to little things like birthday cakes – I cannot even blow out a candle without being triggered by the smell. There are triggers, after triggers, after triggers. Looking back, one of the biggest challenges was the uncertainty. No one knew what was going on. Yes, we all got a phone call to say, *'This is what hotel you're in.'* But no one knew what the plan was for the housing, if missing people were dead or in hospital, or anything. When it came to our living situation, living in temporary accommodation was like being in limbo. At one point, I was literally living out of suitcases, and taking my washing into work. It felt impossible to begin the healing process when everything was still so up in the air.

Aside from the housing instability, there have been so many changes in leadership that it has been difficult to keep track – we have now had two different home secretaries. And they have different priorities, so we – and our inquiry – just keep getting pushed further and further down. It isn't easy to maintain the energy needed to campaign for what we need, while trying to live our own lives as well.

Helping factors

To put it simply, the community was everything. From the very first minute, they were there, whether it came to campaigning, communicating with those making the decisions, or providing very real practical support. After the disaster, there were people everywhere packing boxes, arranging clothing, cooking – there were people from different backgrounds and different ages working openly together. They stood with us. And three and a half years later, they are still by our side. Emotionally, they have been our rock. The Grenfell Wellbeing Service, set up for and by survivors, has also been enormously helpful. I attended the service for around two and a half years to access therapy – the good thing was that there was no limit to the amount of sessions I could access. It was a safe space for me to begin to process all the emotions I had to work through.

Social work response

My family and I were assigned a social worker following the fire, who was our assigned key worker. It is difficult to comment on our relationship because we never actually ended up meeting her – we only spoke over the phone. Which in and of itself was problematic. How can you truly get to know someone over the phone, especially people who had gone through so much? I understand that she was busy, but we did not live on opposite ends of the earth – in fact, we lived five minutes away from her offices. Giving up one hour of an afternoon to put a name to a face would have made a huge difference. I even offered to come to her, but it made no difference.

The truth is, every time I spoke to her, I could hear the stress and burnout in her voice – how much pressure she was under. It just sounded like I was only adding another thing to her to do list. Even when I asked for simple things, they often didn't get done, such as trying to find support to get my university certificates back. It was not a great ask, but it just never happened, so I ended up doing it myself. The only time I managed to get something done really quickly was when I had to shout. But that's not normally me as a person.

On this occasion, we were placed on the eighth floor of a hotel, after asking to be moved for weeks. After everything we had been through, I just could not bear to be placed so high up. Aside from this, there were only two single beds, so there were three of us alternating on the floor – I even slept in the lobby sometimes. Finally, we were moved to an even smaller room. I just absolutely lost it. I am not an aggressive person, but I just phoned my social worker and just screamed. I had just had enough. It was only then that she resolved it. It was what we needed from the start.

On reflection, the fact that she had other work to do on top of supporting families meant that she probably wasn't best placed to respond to the disaster. In future, social workers shouldn't just be pulled from anywhere – there needs to be specialist social workers available to respond to disasters, with an assigned caseload so they can fully dedicate their time to the key worker service.

A lasting message to social workers

If I had one message to give to social workers responding to future disasters, it would be this – it sounds blunt, but if you don't feel you can do it, tell your manager. If you don't feel you can take it on, it is important to own that. You will need to give a lot of emotional support. You're going to have to act fast. You're going to have to expect the unexpected. You're going to hear from a family at five minutes to five who are crying their eyes out. It isn't enough to just want to help. You have to be in the right place to do so, and to deliver a service to the best of your ability.

A lasting message to social work managers

It sounds simple, but it is so important to plan for tomorrow – we never know when another disaster may strike. Have a crystal-clear process to ensure that everyone knows exactly what is expected of them. That way, even if social workers have 101 other things to do, nothing is lost in confusion. Having seen both sides as both a survivor and a trainee social worker, I have a greater understanding of the competing priorities. But systems must be put in place so that survivors can be treated as the priorities they are, rather than a burden or an afterthought.

A tragedy in three acts

Edward Daffarn

Edward Daffarn is a Grenfell survivor who was a resident in Grenfell Tower for 16 years prior to the fire. He is also a registered social worker, specialising in community mental health, and continues to be an active member of Grenfell United.

I would describe Grenfell as a tragedy in three acts. The way we were treated before the fire, the way we were treated on the night of the fire, and the way we have been treated in the aftermath of the fire. In this account, I will focus on the second and third acts – although act one underpins them, because the systemic inequality and social injustice existed long before the tragedy.

The night of the fire was seemingly like any other – I was in bed on the 16th floor of Grenfell Tower, when I heard my neighbour's smoke alarm going off at around 1am. I just assumed he burnt something in the kitchen. But about five or ten minutes later, I heard a commotion outside my door. At this time in the morning, that was not normal, so I got up to see what was happening. When I opened the front door, I expected to find my neighbour apologising. But when I opened the door, I saw this black, acrid smoke. As I closed the door again, my heart sank. I knew this was something really serious.

My first kind of thought was to stay put, as we had been historically instructed by our landlord. At that very moment, my phone rang. A neighbour of mine, who had already got out of the building shouted down the phone, 'Get out, get the fuck out.' Those were his exact words. There was something in the way he spoke to me that just made me act. I went to the bathroom, put a wet towel around my mouth, grabbed my keys and my phone which were by the door, and went out into the hallway. And by this time, I could not see beyond the end of my nose. Instead of finding my way to the emergency exit, I stumbled into a wall that had been built as part of refurbishment work. I started panicking, and as I pawed at the wall, I let go of the towel. Within seconds, I began inhaling the smoke. I was on the verge of taking my last breath when a firefighter came through the door and dragged me out into the communal stairwell. Then I just ran for my life.

Now I know that the only reason the firefighter was there was because my next-door neighbour had begged him to rescue his father. Sadly, his father never made it. As I reached safety, I looked up and saw that the building was ablaze. It was so traumatic – I cannot explain it. I was just wailing in my soul as I looked at it. The time now was 1.30am. All this had happened within half an hour! As I waited outside with other survivors, we were told by the police that some buses were going to come and pick us up. But the buses never came.

After an hour or so, an ambulance driver shouted at us, telling us to 'go home'. At about 3am, it was the local community who offered support by opening a local youth centre. That became a focal point – a gathering place for survivors over the coming weeks.

I consider myself one of the lucky ones. I had not lost anyone. But there were people on that day, and for days afterwards, running around different hospitals trying to find out what happened to their loved ones. What I lost was community, possessions – and I am not talking about flashy goods. I mean things that are very sentimental. Photo albums, funeral service sheets, cards from people I have lost over the years, books that my mom gave me, little things like that. Things I cannot replace, which have immense value, are gone. I know I have a right to grieve the loss of my possessions. But at the same time, they are only possessions, whereas other people have lost far more. So, there is a lot of survivor's guilt. There are lots of emotions to be negotiated. On a personal level, it is difficult to even try to begin to process what happened when I am not yet permanently rehomed. I have not started putting together a new life yet. I have a handful of clothes, a handful of possessions. It took me a long time to get a home together in the first place. I am not sure I will ever do that again.

Grenfell still dominates my life three and a half years on, almost from the minute I wake up to when I go to bed. There is no respite from the 24/7 Grenfell. But long-term well-being will be very much linked to whether we gain justice, change and truth. I have no peace of mind until I see tangible change to social policy. We then need truth from the public inquiry and criminal prosecutions to deliver justice. I naively believed that Grenfell was such a tragedy that something would change. But I am not convinced that it is going to happen now.

To illustrate this point, we were very lucky to get support from the Hillsborough families after Grenfell. And I thought that, after they have been denied justice for 28 years, history would not repeat itself. Because it seems that everything that Hillsborough went through means nothing if we have to do the same thing again.

There were countless challenges following the disaster. On the first night after the fire, I was placed in an emergency accommodation hostel room without any windows and no bathroom in my room. It felt like I was back to square one, when I was living in emergency accommodation before I got into Grenfell. And, being separated from the community like that was especially difficult.

I was fortunate that I had my MP's phone number, and she was able to sort it out for me. But I subsequently found out that after I escaped that fate, they just gave the room to someone less able to advocate for themselves. That still fills me with guilt and shame. In terms of what has helped both during and since the fire, the community has been astounding. Both the short-term and long-term responses were pioneered by them. I found my social worker, allocated to me after the fire, to be helpful – although I was in so much shock and trauma that I cannot remember the granular details of how and why. But I do know that she listened to my needs and ensured they were met – I trusted her. She did things 'with' and not 'to' me.

But I am conscious that it must have been difficult for her to juggle her role of supporting Grenfell survivors, as well as her ordinary case load.

This is something I feel should change – in an ideal world, in future disasters, willing, pre-identified social workers should be seconded into a specialist team. This way, they could drop what they are doing and provide an immediate response. Most teams can cope with losing one worker, particularly with an understanding that the worker has been seconded to a tragedy. And ideally, such workers could also be provided with training, training on trauma and disasters. We need a commitment of trauma-informed social workers who are in it for the long haul with disaster survivors – not social workers who will leave after a couple of weeks.

Grenfell United pioneered a multidisciplinary response to the disaster, with a robust organisational structure, regular supervision and a clear mandate of the role and purpose of each team member. This is something organisations could learn from and implement. As time went on following the disaster, the social workers who were 'parachuted in' left, and then when they were replaced with support workers, our experiences became much more variable without the professional social work ethics and values. I observed there was a lack of supervision among the support workers who were assisting us. This underscored to me the importance of the profession.

My advice to social workers assisting in future disasters would be this – go back to the social work core values and ethics, to the very reason you became a social worker in the first place. Building relationships must be at the heart of every move – you will be dealing with very traumatised people. Listen to what they have to say. Be consistent, be there for them. You can stand tall as a social worker and know that, while you cannot replace what has been lost or change what happened, you can deliver a professional response.

The very small little things make a big difference. If you are running ten minutes late for an appointment, drop someone a text to tell them – it takes you two seconds to do it. Or don't assume that you can sit in someone's seat without asking. Good manners and treating people with respect cannot be underestimated. Treat others as you yourself want to be treated.

Conclusion

The voices of people with lived experience of disasters must be at the heart of any social work response for any intervention to be meaningful. Without acknowledging, engaging with and learning from such expertise, social workers risk adding excessive value to the accounts of those in power (and subsequently removing power and agency from bereaved and survivors). The deeply moving and personal accounts in this chapter provide crucial messages to social workers about how best to support individuals and families experiencing unimaginable pain and suffering; the messages contained here provide opportunities for reflection and will undoubtedly linger with the reader long after the book has been put down. The stories highlight not only the diverse nature of disasters which can occur in a UK context, but also disparities between the social work response according to regional resources, staffing levels, contingency plans (or lack thereof) and so on. This disparity supports BASW's view that social work in disaster planning must be embedded into the profession at a national level, underscored by the appropriate government funding and backing. This should include appropriate training for practitioners of all levels. Further information about BASW's social work in disaster campaign, and how to become involved, can be found at www.basw.co.uk/social-work-disasters

Reflective questions

- Upon reading these powerful stories, how can we meaningfully learn from people with lived experience?
- How will reading these first-hand accounts change your practice?

Taking it further

BASW (nd) *CPD Guidance on Social Work Roles Undertaken during Disasters.* [online] Available at: www.basw.org.uk/system/files/resources/181086%20 CPD%20guidance%20on%20disaster%20social%20work%20V2.pdf (accessed 11 January 2022).

Hughes, M (ed) (2019) *A Guide to Statutory Social Work Interventions: The Lived Experience.* London: Red Globe Press.

CHAPTER 4

MY VOICE: EXPERIENCES OF SOCIAL WORKERS

One of the social workers who contributed to this section referred to herself as a 'wallflower'. It is a word which so beautifully captures the nature of so many practitioners, who tend to step back from the sunlight to allow others to shine. In her own words, taking on the role of a wallflower meant '*fading when not needed, and coming to the fore when I felt I was*'.

In this chapter, we invited social workers (as well as those who supported them through disasters) to step out of the shadows in order that their voices may be heard, and in turn, their wisdom captured so that future practitioners may learn from them. Each contributor has, in their own way, shared their account of the disaster, the personal and professional impact of the experience, key challenges, what worked well, and key messages for social workers, managers and directors.

As with the previous chapter, the stories you find below are written in the authors' own time and through the medium they felt would capture their voice best; for some, this meant putting pen to paper, and for others this meant telling their story with an editor who put pen to paper on their behalf, before developing the piece alongside them.

All practitioners know that social work rarely fits neatly into the nine-to-five, and so BASW England is deeply grateful to all those who not only contributed but gave up their precious time to do so within a busy schedule. We trust that each account will be of value to practitioners of all levels who wish to broaden their knowledge and understanding of such a complex and diverse area of practice.

Self-care

Some readers may find some content distressing. We advise that you take all the time you need when reading, with regular breaks, and reach out for support if needed.

Simply being available

Elizabeth Stevens

Elizabeth Stevens is a social work manager who was called out to respond to the 2017 Manchester Arena bombings. At 10.31pm on Monday 22 May a suicide bomber detonated an explosive device in the foyer of Manchester Arena as people were leaving the arena following a concert by American singer Ariana Grande. Below, Elizabeth reflects on how the disaster impacted on her both personally and professionally, and how it has influenced her practice forever.

Manchester Arena bombing

Following an explosion on 22 May 2017, 22 people were murdered in the Manchester Arena at the end of a pop concert performed by the American artist Ariana Grande. As well as the tragic loss of life, hundreds of people were injured both physically and psychologically. The explosion was caused by the detonating of a bomb in the foyer of the arena where many parents and others were waiting to collect members of the audience who were predominately children, young people and women. Sir John Saunders, in the first volume of the report into the public inquiry describes the event as a *'wicked act inspired by the distorted ideology of the so-called Islamic State'* (2021, p 1). The public inquiry into the Manchester Arena bombing is ongoing.

What can I say? What did I do? It almost feels like putting anything down is disrespectful, making the experience about me, rather than those families on that terrible day... does that make sense? As a social worker, I am so used to hearing and dealing with so much that I sometimes feel a fraud for welling up, as I am right now writing this, thinking about that day and the days after.

It was a day that changed my life forever, both personally and profession- ally. At least 800 people are known to have physical or psychological injuries following on from that night. Twenty-two people died. Twenty-two fam- ilies lost their loved ones. Many others were affected – young people and their families who were enjoying the show, the staff on duty at the arena, the ambulance, police and fire crews, hospital staff, local communities and more.

The majority of the time, I am successful at hiding the experience away in a little box – but small things, such as walking past the Manchester Arena, or hearing the poem 'This is the Place', bring emotions flooding back.

In the first few hours and days after the disaster, there were many of us who rallied together and provided what the city needed from us. I arrived at the Etihad football stadium just before 7am, taking over from a colleague who had been up all night. I was the on-call manager for the Bronze team (Gold, Silver and Bronze are terms used in civil contingencies). I ended up staying for 15 hours. The space had been dedicated to supporting lost and scared families who were unable to find loved ones.

I can still visualise the room – a large, luxurious space, somewhere that used to be filled with laughter, camaraderie and mostly joy (depending on the football performance of course). I can still picture the families and friends in their groups. I can still hear and feel the noise and pain of grief as it cried out of people. I can remember my stomach responding physically to the noise of human pain and anguish.

On that day and in that moment, I was calm. In social work, there is something about being in control when presented with the uncontrollable and adapting to the situation in front of you. You forget how much you notice in a single glance as a social worker. On that day, as I stood respectfully watching from the refreshment centre (which became the focal point of the room), I noticed a lot. I knew how people took their tea and coffee, I saw someone running out of cigarettes so went to get some for her, a family member was vegan, so I arranged for her to have a vegan meal. I passed phone chargers around, discreetly placing them close to families, so they were there if needed.

My thinking at the time was that if we could get people's basic needs met, along with the other volunteers, they would be better able to manage whatever news was coming their way. In a crisis like this, the day-to-day skills of a social worker you use without thinking, such as empathy, flexibility, communication, being approachable and resourceful, equip you to manage and deliver what is needed. Being a wallflower was one of the most important skills I used on the day, which meant fading when not needed, and coming to the fore when I felt I was. At the time, I did not realise I was assessing the situation over and over, but I was. If I noticed tension, heightened emotion, or anger about the lack of information, I would try to intervene by topping up drinks, replacing tissues or removing cups.

I was simply being available to different individuals in different ways.

I spoke to one man who saw what happened first-hand. He said he knew the situation was hopeless, but he could not talk to his family so he talked to me. Others wanted to talk about the ordinary – the weather, the football stadium; others wanted to tell you about their family member or friend and something funny they had shared; others sought out a physical connection and hugged me tight in response to what they perceived as an act of kindness.

After the disaster, we were offered a peer talking session facilitated by a counsellor through our employee assistance programme. About six months later, we had a learning event designed to help us reflect on what happened, to understand what worked well, what could have gone better, and how the disaster had impacted on us. This timeframe was useful as it provided the time and space needed to look back from a distance. The one-to-one support I received in the aftermath helped enormously – there truly was an open-door policy. My line manager, someone who is naturally intuitive and highly supportive, was one person I could talk to whenever I needed to – knowing I could do so really helped. In the weeks after, she was supportive, appreciative, and flexible as I began to slowly process what had happened.

My professional supervisor at that time took a different strategy with me. In supervision, she held a mirror to me, asking challenging questions about how

I was coping, and what my outlets were. She suggested I had not dealt with what had occurred. While this was difficult and awkward, in doing so, she provided me with an opportunity to be honest with myself, about my need to take some time, and make some space to begin dealing with emotions (whether on the tram, in the bath, or wherever else). This reflection made me realise that some emotions still clung to me and were bubbling just under the surface. Being prompted to be honest about my need to deal with the incident was the vehicle which enabled me to do so. This is something I now apply when supervising others.

If I were to give practitioners one piece of advice, it would be this: When you are faced with it, be a swan, trust yourself. Find your inner core. Take a deep breath, you can and will deal with it. My advice to social work managers and organisation would be this: In all the chaos that goes alongside a disaster, look after the basic needs of the social workers, as well as your own, starting with the lowest rung on Maslow's hierarchy. In a disaster such as this, you can only do what you can to help people be more ready to survive. Above all, trust the social worker to do the job you need them to do when it comes to human beings. Believe in the strength of your practitioners. Ensure that people have an outlet for their trauma, so that it does not weigh down on their shoulders.

There is no doubt that I am changed as a practitioner. I am more confident in my ability to manage in a crisis, and in fact, to manage most situations that come my way. I have a better understanding of the impact of vicarious trauma, and how much we generally take on as practitioners. While the disaster was an extreme circumstance, it made me reflect on our discipline as a whole and how strong and resilient we are. We take on the risk, the anger, frustration and the joy. We walk alongside the people we are involved with. It is a privileged place.

When 'normal' was suspended

Janet Foulds

Janet Foulds is a social worker, practice manager, and a visiting profes-sional fellow in Social Work at the University of Derby, who was part of the social work disaster recovery response for both the Hillsborough football disaster and the Kegworth air crash (1989). In the piece below she reflects on how both incidents continue to impact her practice, and shares some of the key learning she took from these painful experiences.

Kegworth air disaster

Travelling from Heathrow, London, to Belfast, Northern Ireland, on 8 January 1989, a British Midlands Boeing 737-400 aeroplane encountered engine problems. The plane was diverted to East Midlands Airport but came down on an embankment of the M1 motorway in Kegworth, Leicestershire. There were 126 people on board and 47 were killed with a further 74 injured. The incident was due to a pilot error. Lessons from the Kegworth disaster have resulted in improved practices in airline safety. This includes the adoption of the brace position in the event of an emergency as standard protocol and the introduction of pictorial safety briefing cards behind each seat in an aeroplane (Sommerlad, 2019).

Disasters, by their very nature, are sudden, unpredictable and intense events which interrupt normal life. Each is unique. Some are small in scope and locally contained while others affect whole communities or even countries. The Aberfan mining disaster (1966) devastated an entire community. The attack on the World Trade Center (2001) killed and injured thousands of people and its impact was felt around the globe.

Every day social workers in practice encounter what many people would describe as personal disasters: life-changing events like serious illness, bereavements, being victims of crime. Our work brings us into people's lives, and in doing so we experience at very close quarters the joys, challenges and tragedies of life.

Until faced with the reality of a major incident or disaster we cannot know how each of us might react if called upon to help. As social workers we are professionally trained and skilled at helping people experiencing distress or trauma in their lives. We receive professional supervision and support to assist us in our work and that goes some way to ensure that we can cope with the demands the work makes on us and so avoid becoming overwhelmed by the pain of others.

Although it is a challenge for many social workers in these highly pressured, resource-scarce times, we hope to enjoy a fulfilling private life knowing that we have made a real difference in our work. However, disasters bring their own challenges. A major incident may directly affect the area where we live and work and may even harm our own relatives, friends and colleagues.

Here, I reflect on my experiences as a social worker involved in two major disasters. Both of the events happened over 30 years ago but the memories remain sharp. There have been many experiences during my social work career that could appropriately warrant the description of 'disasters' but I hope that my personal experiences relating specifically to the Kegworth and Hillsborough disasters will prove a helpful contribution for social work colleagues who find themselves working in similar crisis situations. I offer these thoughts with humility as my experience of disaster work is limited but I hope they will encourage others to meet the challenge if faced with similar crises.

Kegworth air crash (1989)

A British Midland aeroplane flying from London Heathrow to Belfast International airport crashed onto a motorway embankment between the M1 motorway and A453 road near Kegworth, Leicestershire, England while attempting an emergency landing at East Midlands Airport. There were 126 passengers and crew on board; 39 people died at the scene. The death toll later rose to 47. Seventy per cent of the people on the plane came from Northern Ireland. Casualties were taken to hospitals in three different Midland counties: Leicestershire, Nottinghamshire and Derbyshire. There were over 400 relatives from Northern Ireland in the area following the crash.

In the immediate aftermath of the crash, social workers had a number of roles including in hospitals, with the injured in wards and in receiving centres to meet families arriving in the area. We were allocated to families and assisted them in a number of ways, practically and emotionally. Social workers were involved with families of the bereaved and with those whose relatives had survived but who were badly injured in hospital. We were there to care for, support and advocate on behalf of the families.

I was completely unprepared for what was to come that night. The plane crash occurred on a Sunday evening. I was at home living very close to the main hospital in the city of Derby. On hearing about the crash, I thought that social workers might be needed, so I volunteered to help.

There was a time lag between the crash and casualties arriving at the hospital. At first, all seemed eerily quiet and calm. That was soon to change. In the time it took to call home to get changed and return to the hospital, perhaps half an hour, a huge crowd had gathered, and it was difficult to get through the police barrier to report to the on-duty social work manager. Thankfully, he was able to confirm that I was a social worker.

Initially, I was based at the local hospital meeting families, gathering information, arranging accommodation and transport, later accompanying relatives to the airport hotel where the temporary mortuary had been set up. We accompanied the police and were asked to be with relatives as they received bad news and as they identified the deceased. For some families many hours elapsed between the crash and hearing confirmation of the death of their loved ones. We stayed with them while they waited and afterwards to offer what comfort we could.

My role was relatively short term – during the night of the disaster, during the following day and for the week afterwards where further work was needed in the hospital. Nevertheless the experience for me and my colleagues was distressing and challenging. Disasters take on a life of their own and I soon began to realise that I was about to be a part of something quite unprecedented and well outside of my previous social work experience.

Hillsborough football stadium disaster (1989)

Ninety-seven Liverpool football fans died as a result of crush injuries and 766 people were injured at an FA cup semi-final football match between Liverpool and Nottingham Forest. The match was due to be played at Hillsborough, Sheffield Wednesday's ground in South Yorkshire. As a result, people directly affected by the incident came from a very wide geographical area. The Taylor Report followed, criminal proceedings against the police and club officials were instigated and the campaign for justice by the Hillsborough families continues to this day.

Social workers from Derbyshire were asked by the then director of social services to travel to Sheffield to assist colleagues in whatever way we could. I agreed to go and was really glad to be able to travel with my colleague with whom I had worked at Kegworth. It had been a fine spring afternoon. How quickly that would change.

The football ground became the centre of the police operation at Hillsborough so the 'reception centre' was in real contrast to conditions at Kegworth where the airline had provided comfortable private rooms and refreshments for families and responders at the airport hotel.

In Sheffield a lot of activity happened at the football ground in a large gymnasium which served many purposes, as a reception centre for relatives, a base for the police investigation as well as housing the temporary mortuary. When we arrived at the ground it was dark. I remember the gymnasium was cold and noisy – a far cry from the more comfortable and altogether softer surroundings of the airport hotel. Reflecting on both disasters I learned how important the environment is in offering care and comfort to grieving families. At Kegworth families were offered privacy. At Hillsborough it appeared that everything was happening under the same roof, thus greatly increasing everyone's exposure to trauma.

We accompanied relatives as they were asked to identify their loved ones from photographs. This involved having to look at photographs of all of the deceased – a truly traumatic experience for everyone concerned. I remember thinking that the walk of a few feet from one end of the photo board to the other would change those people's lives for ever and it did. We stayed with relatives as they formally identified the bodies which were brought out from the curtained off mortuary at one end of the gym, another harrowing experience for the bereaved.

My role at the Hillsborough disaster was relatively short in terms of time but social work colleagues from Sheffield and Liverpool worked with families over a much longer period of time offering a range of services and support. My colleague, Jenny Liew, and I were able later to attend the memorial service in Liverpool where we met with colleague social workers who were based in Liverpool and who were working with families on their return home.

Preparation and impact

The experience from Kegworth helped considerably as we had some idea of what might happen and what we might have to face. I was able to prepare a little more, thinking about what I might need to take. It is really important to remember to have money, suitable clothing, food and drink during what can be an indeterminate period of time. More importantly, I was able to buddy up with my colleague, Jenny, with whom I had worked so closely during the Kegworth incident. This support was invaluable and we could plan together what we were going to do and how we would look out for each other during our time in Sheffield and beyond.

The year 1989 was tough, but I do not regret the experiences. A passenger aircraft exploded over Lockerbie, Scotland on 21 December 1988, after a bomb was detonated. The Lockerbie air crash occurred two weeks before the Kegworth plane went down. It is a long time ago, but the memories are still clear and powerful, and I learned so much. The two experiences occurred quite close together in early 1989. At the same time, in my day job in Children's Services, we were also learning about some pretty frightening child sexual abuse cases as well as dealing with our normal workload. It is fair to say that involvement in both disasters had a considerable impact on me both personally and professionally.

Following the Kegworth disaster, research undertaken by Dr Marion Gibson (2006) highlights that responders share frustration at the lack of information, share the pain and sorrow of the bereaved, and share the sense of relief when relatives have survived. They share the weariness and stress of fellow responders. I can relate to all of that. We were faced with desperate relatives clamouring for information and were frustrated that we could not provide clear and accurate facts. We were exposed to sights, sounds and experiences that were shocking, difficult and intense. Listening to details of injuries, looking at photographs of deceased people and the experience of seeing multiple dead bodies is emotionally difficult even if one had previously experienced bereavements.

Witnessing people in such pain was harrowing for us and our professional problem-solving instincts were very severely limited in those circumstances. Faced with grief and bereavement on a large scale we had to rely on our personal resources of care, kindness, empathy and compassion. The families needed us to stay with their powerful emotions and grief rather than trying to find a solution or think we could make it better which we obviously were unable to do. People's reactions were wide-ranging and difficult to predict. Some were silent and numb. Others screamed and raged. Some ran in a vain attempt to distance themselves from the horror of what they had been told.

As helpers we could not easily separate ourselves from the shocking reality of multiple fatalities and casualties or cut off from the emotional trauma we saw, heard and experienced. We could offer comfort, but we couldn't bring their loved ones back. Inevitably, people from a very wide geographical area would be affected by these tragedies. Marion Gibson describes the *'ripple effect'*. For some responders the emotional fallout affected their own lives for some considerable time after the event.

There were many challenges. Although we know that social work can be unpredictable, as practitioners we usually expect to plan our involvement and there are boundaries to our work. Many of us work within organisational structures with clear managerial lines and accountability procedures and processes. Major incidents do not obey the rules or stick to boundaries. Emergency planning has made enormous progress over the years, but it is inevitable, however good the planning, that disasters are likely to be characterised by some degree of chaos and disorganisation.

The Kegworth response drew workers from three counties, so responders were working outside of their familiar organisational structures. Many of the normal organisational and reporting structures cannot be in place when disasters occur. We found ourselves working outside normal hours, away from home and away from normal supports. 'Normal' was suspended and we had to work collaboratively with colleagues from several agencies. Teamwork was essential.

Identifying ourselves as social workers was a challenge. Most responders wore clearly identifiable uniforms. WRVS (Women's Royal Voluntary Service, now known as the Royal Voluntary Service) volunteers, the Salvation Army and other faith representatives were easy to spot. Unfortunately, at that time, all we had were small identity cards. These were of little use in a large-scale disaster. Social workers need to be clearly identifiable. Derbyshire now issues social workers with tabards, which are much more visible in a crowd.

As we approached these events it is fair to say that all senses were heightened, and feelings magnified. We were anxious as we didn't know what we would face. On both occasions we knew there would be many casualties and possibly multiple fatalities. How would we cope?

In our societies, death is usually sensitively managed and dealt with in quite orderly, private and clinical ways. This was very different and many of the normal rituals associated with death and bereavement were missing. It was not easy to work out who oversaw what and it was not clear to whom, as social workers, we were supposed to report. We were not sure what our role was to be, and this knowledge is vitally important if we are to avoid becoming helpless bystanders at an incident.

The Kegworth and Hillsborough disasters happened before the widespread availability of personal mobile phones and this provided a major challenge as we were faced with a high number of distressed people, all desperate for information and also frantic to contact family members. There were insufficient telephones at Hillsborough. Hopefully, that would not be the case now, but it is important to acknowledge that in some disasters mobile phone networks and communication infrastructure may be severely affected or totally disabled. As well as professional responders, major incidents also attract many volunteers. Organising everyone becomes a logistical challenge.

When we arrived in Sheffield, we tried to report to whoever was in charge of directing operations but, in the confusion and absence of clear instructions, we used our initiative and went directly to the football stadium where we thought we could be of some use.

An added challenge at both incidents was the inevitable media interest. In our day-to-day social work, it is fair to say that most of us try to avoid the media spotlight to protect confidentiality and especially given the harsh treatment meted out to our profession over the years. Unless we are formally representing our profession through BASW or have the permission of employers, most of us normally do not have to engage directly with the media but disasters are extremely newsworthy, and publicity is inevitable. It is important that social workers understand who is to manage the media response and are careful not to speak inadvertently. I learned how certain members of the media operate. Some were genuine and courteous, of course, but others were quite devious. I recall being at the hospital with a family who just wanted a breath of fresh air. As we stood outside, we realised we were being filmed. During the time spent at the hospital we also encountered reporters attempting to gain access to families by pretending to be medical staff. We felt protective towards the families, learned to be very careful about who we spoke to and were able to advise accordingly.

It is a reminder that on occasions like this, despite the chaos, our work remains open to scrutiny and publicity and as professionals we remain accountable at all times. As is the case with Hillsborough, criminal proceedings can follow a tragedy and I was surprised very recently to be contacted by police who wished to interview those who were helping in Sheffield. The interview was part of the most recent criminal proceedings against the police match commander. One doesn't normally expect to be interviewed after so many years. Not surprisingly, recalling events of that night in forensic detail brought back many of the feelings associated with the disaster.

Neither was I prepared, following the plane crash, for the arrival at the reception centre of the then prime minister, Margaret Thatcher, and her entourage. From watching numerous news reports I understand that this is fairly normal practice but, sitting quietly with a couple whose daughter had just died, I remember feeling angry on their behalf by the intrusive nature of the TV cameras, microphones and bright lights – an unwanted intrusion into private grief. Maybe some families derived comfort from this visit, but I was not convinced.

Worse still, the Hillsborough disaster took place in the full glare of publicity as the football match was televised live. No doubt that added hugely to the trauma experienced by the families of those injured and deceased. For various reasons the disaster has remained in the media spotlight for 30 years – because of the ongoing campaign for justice by the Hillsborough families, the ongoing criminal proceedings and the fact that whenever Hillsborough comes into the news there are replays and distressing clips of the event shown without warning. Memories come flooding back. The Liverpool families have used and continue positively to use the media to bring attention to their fight for justice, but it must be remembered how the images from the disaster shown repeatedly on news bulletins can retraumatise families and responders alike.

One particular challenge presents itself for social workers and other responders after any disaster. That is, how to return to 'normal' work and routines after such intense experiences. Strong bonds are formed with families in a very short time. Knowing when to stay and when to leave is a challenge and it isn't always easy for workers to 'let go' especially when you have been alongside people for hours and days through intense and life-changing moments. Workers may need help to do this and will benefit from time out from normal duties for a while in order to recover and process what they have been a part of. It is important to be particularly sensitive to the needs of colleagues who may have experienced vicarious trauma as a result of their involvement as this, if not addressed, may negatively affect a worker's ability to function well in their normal job.

What helped during the disaster?

My experience as a children and families social worker helped. Having an understanding of people's needs and reactions at times of trauma and loss was an advantage as was my previous experience in mental health work.

Throughout my career I have been fortunate to be able to rely on incredible support from family, friends and social work colleagues. That has sustained me through decades of social work. Of particular importance for me at the two disasters was the support of a close colleague. We were able to buddy up and take care of each other during and after the events.

I remember small acts of kindness that meant a lot – people providing drinks and snacks to help us to keep going over many hours. I was aware that helpers were supporting and taking care of each other – offering a comforting touch and words of encouragement, advising colleagues to take a break.

It was helpful to have some understanding about the roles that different responders had and my previous experience of working together with colleagues in a multidisciplinary way was valuable. Having a clear understanding of everyone's roles and responsibilities allows people to get on with their work unimpeded.

What helped since the disaster?

In more recent times being a member of a crisis response team has provided opportunities to undertake joint training and to learn, reflect and hear about responses to other major incidents.

Following Kegworth and Hillsborough I was mindful of the need to avoid traumatising friends and family by recounting what happened but there was a need to talk and share feelings engendered by the events.

It is very helpful to have a safe space to talk with colleagues who have shared the same or similar experiences.

Although there are differing views about critical incident debriefing, I found it was helpful after the events to attend a debrief. This happened immediately at the hospital as we returned from Kegworth, and further meetings were arranged in the weeks that followed. This served to acknowledge our contribution to helping families and provided opportunities to talk freely.

Being part of the Derbyshire Crisis Response Team provided guidance, support, and some very valuable training about aspects of disaster management. I am grateful for the support and guidance provided by Paula McDonald, senior emergency planning officer, Derbyshire County Council.

Training

The following are ideas for really useful training for social workers based on Derbyshire's Emergency Planning Team approach.

- Multi-agency training regarding roles and responsibilities of various professionals and volunteers.
- Information about how police manage major incidents, management of crime scenes and the role of the family liaison officer.
- Understanding the legal processes in relation to coroners' procedures and release of bodies (relatives were distressed by not being able to touch or hold the deceased in both disasters).
- Learning from other disasters.
- Learning about the psychological impact of disasters on responders and implications for returning safely to family and normal work duties.
- Management of information during the incident.
- Safeguarding responsibilities in a disaster.
- Media policy and protocols.
- Hospital protocols when working with casualties.
- Dealing with pets.
- Requirements for recording work undertaken at an incident.

- Understanding bereavement, loss, mourning and grief reactions.
- Cultural issues to consider relating to death and funerals.
- Understanding stress reactions, post-traumatic stress disorder (PTSD) and what help is needed in the immediate aftermath and longer term.

What have I learnt?

The experience taught me about myself and what I can cope with and confirmed for me why I became a social worker. I realised that there were no comprehensive sets of instruction for times like these, no scripts to follow. Everyone involved has to be prepared to work flexibly and respond to what is before them while being clear and confident about their respective professional roles.

This was not a time primarily for problem-solving although there were numerous practical issues to deal with. People needed help in a range of ways. Being with grieving relatives over many hours brings a roller-coaster of emotions. There are moments of acute distress, interspersed with quiet reflection and even moments of laughter as people talk about and recall happy memories of their loved ones.

We give freely of ourselves, our time, our compassion and our empathy. A person-centred approach is needed and the term *'use of self'* takes on much greater significance. Being so closely involved with grieving relatives was physically and emotionally draining. Empathy can hurt. We are exposed to some painful experiences, and it was inevitable that we experience feelings of bereavement as a result of helping.

Returning to normal routines after such intense experiences is difficult. For some time, the thoughts and memories are preoccupying and emotions are pretty near the surface.

I know that I became less tolerant of what I see as the over-bureaucratisation of our profession. What people need at the very worst time of their lives is for someone to be with them, stay with them and, most importantly, to listen. They need comfort and an empathic human response; closeness and touch with appropriate professional boundaries, not distance; communication but with fewer words.

Our involvement at both incidents was acknowledged and appreciated by our employers and councillors and that was really helpful, as was the support we received from colleagues. Our experiences were put to good use in training.

BASW's work on highlighting the role of social workers in disasters has been excellent and supportive, giving a clear message that social workers have a role in responding to disasters and confirming the view that this is a valuable part of social work.

As members of the Derby and Derbyshire Crisis Response Team, we have had the benefit of access to training and useful exercises – eg, rest centre/role play exercises, introductory course (one day), core skills course (three days). Update sessions are provided during the year with a focus on specialist topics.

Less helpful, perhaps, was the lack of understanding of the impact of the disasters on our ability to return quickly to our normal day jobs. This was not intentional but I think we underestimated how we would feel.

Employers need to do what they can to enable social workers to practise safely in disaster situations and to be aware of the potential impact on practitioners as, left unaddressed, these issues may cause problems in day-to-day work. Other emergency services do this routinely.

Members of the Derbyshire Crisis Response Team are drawn from children- or adult-focused social care and voluntary agencies. Their skills, experience and knowledge include the ability to:

- relate to people in acute distress including those facing bereavement;
- assess the immediate practical and emotional needs of people involved in an incident;
- undertake welfare tasks while responding to emotional needs;
- work on their own initiative in rapidly changing situations;
- work with other responders from police, health, and voluntary services; and
- understand their own needs when working under potentially very difficult circumstances.

If I could give social workers one message it would be: Remember what you came into the work for. Social workers have the skills transferable to disaster work. Although this is not for everyone, we definitely have a role. We need to be clear what that role is. Flexibility and sensitivity are essential in an effective social work response. As with many areas of social work practice, teamwork is essential. We have a duty to work collaboratively, be clear about our roles and respect the roles of others. Each has a crucial part to play.

Take care to have sufficient support. If you do not feel able to take part in the disaster response it is important to say so. We owe it to our families and to the people needing help not to become casualties ourselves. The stress of day-to-day social work is often underestimated. Insufficient attention is given to this in our practice which can leave otherwise competent professionals in trouble and may be a contributory factor in the high turnover of staff. Social work makes considerable demands on personal resources at a basic human level. Disasters have the power to traumatise and overwhelm us if we do not understand this.

There is potential for any person helping at a disaster to experience feelings of shock, powerlessness, grief, exhaustion and intrusive memories – a parallel process of trauma and bereavement. Professionals exposed to this will be personally affected. This highlights the value of staff care and reflective practice not just for disaster work but to help us to practise safely in our day-to-day work.

Working together with colleagues from other agencies and disciplines is essential and the more we understand about each other's roles the better the response. For example, understanding the roles of police, the coroner and health protocols is vitally important. Also, understanding the various rites and rituals surrounding death and funerals, including faith and cultural differences. Most importantly, in an emergency situation social workers need to understand the chain of command during the incident and the boundaries of their work. *We are there to be a part of a team.*

Despite the chaos associated with disasters, social workers remain accountable for their work. We are accountable for what we do, say and record and we need to be aware of protocols and legal issues surrounding investigations. Many years after the Hillsborough tragedy we were required to be interviewed about our work in 1989 as part of a criminal investigation.

Messages to social work managers and organisations

- Ensure that multi-agency planning is in place, recognising the role of social work in disasters.

- Remember your duty of care to staff, including offering appropriate training and support to avoid emotional harm.

- Consider what plans to put into place for staff after the event or incident including time off work, debriefing events and counselling.

- While the nature of disasters is unpredictable, equip social workers so that they are prepared and able to cope in these situations.

- Ensure that everyone knows about the emergency planning process in your area, including follow-up arrangements for professionals taking part.

Disasters bring chaos on a large scale and, thankfully, this is not what we routinely have to cope with in our daily lives. However, disasters are not uncommon, and it is best to be as prepared as we can be in our service response. Whatever the circumstances, survivors and their relatives need us to be with them at possibly the worst and most distressing time of their lives, ensuring safety but mostly listening and offering comfort.

Strip away the normal trappings of our work and what we have left to draw on during critical incidents are the human qualities so essential at times of acute distress: calmness, care, compassion, comfort, acceptance and empathy, while providing practical help and guidance. Counselling may be helpful for people in the longer term if they choose to use it but in the immediate after-math of a critical incident and where there are mass fatalities there are few words to use. We are there to offer support to people who are in shock and great distress.

Computer-dominated practice and the trend towards hot desking have reduced considerably the opportunities for team support. In my opinion, this increases isolation and does not address the need to nurture social work staff, especially newly qualified practitioners. Social workers need to be trained, supported and equipped to be working effectively as part of a team – good practice at disasters relies on shared planning, shared training and, vitally important, willingness to work collaboratively with colleagues from a range of agencies.

Families in distress may not always want our help at the time it is offered but it might be more welcome at a later stage. Being part of a disaster response gives us an opportunity to use our social work skills positively to dispel a few myths surrounding our profession and to make a real difference. It is important to say that I was never so proud to be a social worker when the call came, and it was a privilege to be able to help. I know that social workers made a positive difference for the families who needed our help, and I learned an incredible amount from the experiences which aided both my personal and professional development.

Thirty years may have passed since the Hillsborough and Kegworth disasters but the people I met have never been forgotten.

Her brown eyes

Emma Bint

Emma Bint is a social worker who provided support to vulnerable families during the Covid-19 global pandemic, as part of her statutory placement in Children's Services. Below, she reflects on what it was like to adapt to this new world on the frontline.

At the beginning of the pandemic, our department was responding to a child protection investigation, which led to a child requiring a medical examination. I was in the duty team on that day, which meant I was responding to the incident.

Before we even got to the hospital, we faced difficulties. I had to support the parent's anxieties about attending the hospital. This was difficult to negotiate when the media was informing people only to attend in a crisis. The hospital, it was eerie. The waiting room was like a ghost town, and everyone was draped in full personal protective equipment (PPE). When I met with the child I was supporting, she looked so scared – she was the only one not wearing any PPE. Her brown eyes glared around the room, but no words were spoken.

The doctor tried to speak to her, but her questions were muffled by the face mask. She appeared to be requesting reassurance with her eyes, which didn't arrive. The child was not responding. Suddenly, everyone was looking at me, and even as an adult I found it hard to know what their eyes were asking. I took my mask off, removed my gloves and apron and lowered myself down and touched her hand. She smiled. I said *'Everything is okay. Because of this silly virus, people have to wear these silly masks.'* She laughed and squeezed my hand. I told her that the doctor needed to ask her some questions and that I would hold her hand until she felt comfortable.

The doctor removed her mask, then so did the nurses one by one.

Although we were living and working in unknown territory, this was one of those moments when you realise that there are more things to consider than your own safety. What is truly important in life is supporting other people who are more scared than you are.

Masked Faces

A poem by Emma Bint

So many people
Why were they here?
I had told my story
But I wasn't in fear.

I was taken to hospital
Where people in gowns
Covered their faces
Was this to cover their frowns?

They expected me to talk
I was fearful now
These people didn't seem human
And I felt lost in the crowd.

$\longrightarrow$

I spotted some friendly eyes
That were warm and kind
It was that lovely lady by whom I was mesmerised.

She took off her mask
And held my hand
Now I am not fearful
And am able to be found.

The others followed
Faces could be seen.
The friendly lady helped me to feel at ease.

I told my story
It was easier now
The lovely lady she knew how.

We are social beings

Joanne Bush

Joanne Bush is an advanced practitioner in Gateway to Care at Calderdale Council in the UK. Below, she discusses how her team adapted to the Covid-19 crisis at both a professional and personal level, reflecting on the positive learning which can be applied to a post-pandemic world.

Due to Covid-19, our team was repurposed overnight, and staff redeployed to a 'Social Care Hub' – a single point of contact for anyone needing support directly due to Covid-19, such as shopping, medication collection, emotional or mental health support. My experience of a whole team being repurposed during 'normal times' is that it would take several weeks, if not months to navigate systemic and organisational barriers. However, in this time of crisis, the usual complications and conflict that mar this kind of multi-agency work were replaced by co-ordinated co-operation and we were quickly able to tap into existing community resources to provide support all over the Calderdale valley. Reflecting on this has made me think how quickly the unimaginable can suddenly be imagined and how easy it *could* be for organisations to work together towards a single aim in 'normal' times.

My role within this hub was to respond to requests for support, and screen referrals which I then sent through to the relevant volunteer hubs. I have spoken to many people with diverse experiences and life situations. People who have never imagined they would ever use food banks have had to ask for help with feeding their families, and it is clear that the people who are already economically disadvantaged are more devastated by the impact of Covid-19. I have heard stories of resilience, stoicism and kindness and I have heard stories of anxiety, fear and distress. Some people have given up all their free time to support more vulnerable members of the community; others will not even sit in their garden for fear of catching Covid-19. One thing I have taken from this echoed learning from my previous practice, supporting people who were dying, is that we cannot control what happens, we can only control how we respond to it. Focusing on kindness and compassion in the face of adversity can bring profound moments of joy. But a focus on your fear and anxiety can impact all aspects of your health and well-being.

We have been calling the physical distance between us 'social distancing', but it has been anything but this. We are social beings and need each other in times like this. Most people are kind; but they are also complicated, and those complexities mean that what we do in times of crisis doesn't seem to be able to be replicated without an imminent fear looming. Rather than complacently assuming that things will go on this way forever, we need to remember things can be different and we do not need a disaster to change things. We need to take the things that have been positive from this wake-up call (communities uniting, people working together, time spent with loved ones) and remember how quickly we *can* change those aspects of society that do not serve our communities and the vulnerable people we support.

Grenfell: the worst moment of my professional life

Lucy Easthope

Professor Lucy Easthope is a leading authority on recovering from disaster, who was an advisor following the Grenfell Tower fire, 14 June 2017. Her areas of research include mass fatalities planning, legal aspects of emergencies, identifying lessons post-incident, the effectiveness of public inquiries, interoperability and community resilience in practice. She is a co-founder of the After Disaster Network, University of Durham, which was set up to examine learning from these major tragedies. Below, Lucy reflects on her personal and professional response to the disaster, advises on how best to support practitioners, and discusses what she learned from both frontline social workers and survivors about best practice in disaster contexts.

The realisation that Grenfell was happening was devastating – it was the worst moment of my professional life. It was obvious from the early hours of 14 June that this would be incredibly complex, and a terrible tragedy. In many ways, any disaster simply highlights existing problems and cracks in the system; whatever else is going on in society at that time is highly relevant. My immediate concern was about support and resources because there had been so many cuts to them. I knew that this was going to be very difficult for the community and authorities to respond to. There was, of course, the context of austerity, which social work is highly vulnerable to, not only in terms of larger caseloads but also in terms of being both affected by and responsive to societal change.

There were a number of factors that I feared would make it a worst-case scenario. People were extremely traumatised by what they had seen that night and what they had lost. There was a collective sense of bereavement throughout the wider community. To lose that number of people and in such circumstances. I work a lot with forensic colleagues and I knew that social workers that went in would be working with families who had lost loved ones, but may have had no chance to see a deceased loved one. I am a national advisor on disaster mortuary provision and the care of the deceased and the bereaved, so I had a real sense of the challenge at that point.

I wasn't sure what the role of the social workers would automatically look like. London had well developed plans for supporting families in the days after disaster but there were a number of problems here that are currently being examined by the public inquiry, and much of the community felt abandoned. Logistically there was a challenge because many local areas contract with charities like the British Red Cross to provide family contact points, but a large proportion of the responders had been sent to Manchester for a terrorist attack three weeks earlier.

Then we heard the call for the development of a 'key worker' service, utilising London's social workers. Almost immediately they were given quite a significant portfolio which saw them deploying into areas that I had previously seen held by police family liaison officers (FLOs). I had lobbied government for more training for social workers for this scenario, supporting the families through the policing process after loss etc, but had always been told by central government that police FLOs would do it.

The fire took place in an area of huge community resilience, but equally in a place where there were high levels of deprivation and child poverty. There is a significant social disparity between North Kensington and South Kensington (Gentleman, 2017). An additional factor was that many families required translation services and other support, which meant responding was highly complex. Aside from any language barriers, there were also cultural differences to consider. Up until that point, the British approach to emergency planning had assumed a very white British model of response. When I think back, few of our traditional messages would have landed. As an example, a lot of UK literature responded to the importance of insurance, which is problematic in the context of Islam. All our mental health checklists ask about alcohol use. Some government forms used such specific terminology that they made no sense if translated into another language.

I learnt so much more about practices, harms and clumsiness. At one point, families were given John Lewis cards to replace the cookware they had lost. Some of the Eritrean and Somali families, who had lost everything, were saying 'We lost what we brought over – you can't get that in John Lewis'.

When it came to communicating with diverse survivors, social workers were the most humbling to watch. Many of them were local to the area and such passionate advocates. They were incredible translators of what worked, the right practices, and how to communicate. They couldn't just reach for existing tools or checklists because so many of them were inappropriate. Many of the government documents for the immediate post-disaster stage use terms like 'regeneration' and that was a highly controversial term. It had become synonymous with gentrification and being forced out, so all of those documents could not be used. I have never seen such fast document turnaround and sharing.

Social work response

Looking back, it was almost as if I was a bag of broken pottery in the first year; responding to Grenfell broke me down. It was the social workers and the charity workers and the community and families who rebuilt me but also taught me. I had responded to many 'mass fatalities' incidents by then, and many had similarities, but this was an incredibly hard environment. Decisions by central government were so at odds with established disaster principles that I had to constantly shift and reshape any preconceived ideas (Eyre and Dix, 2014).

I was used to a big toolkit of existing leaflets and documents but all of those had to be rewritten and rethought.

The individual social work responses that I saw were phenomenal. Frontline workers taught me about understanding cultural competency (and incompetency) and considerations in a way I thought I understood but had not truly lived through until that point. They constantly required me to think, learn and innovate. To check. Events would be scheduled and then I would double check and they would clash with an important religious holiday. My message there would be to always check and to ask the community and their advocates, which is what many of the key workers were.

It made me realise what it takes to be a social worker in modern Britain.

The social workers who responded to Grenfell were very, very aware of their responsibility. And one of the things that was very useful to learn was that they stayed as social workers throughout the response. I was constantly in awe of their professional decision-making and professional boundaries. They understood supervision and escalation better than any other response I have worked on. I have trained what are called 'care teams' or 'crisis teams' for organisations all over the world. People who are brought in to help families, just for the first few weeks. Here it was clear that the 'key worker' service would stay for much longer, with a bigger remit than I had seen before. The social workers poured every ounce of their past experience into the response.

Often, as a consultant, I am brought in to teach and train. And of course, that is something that happened – but it was a true exchange of knowledge and learning. I taught social workers about the return of personal effects, victim identification processes, things to think about in a post-disaster community space. They were teaching me about the structural racism that is faced constantly, and the bureaucracy that families face. It also taught me to communicate so much better. I spend a lot of time with police and other emergency planners and you can slip so easily into a world of assumed knowledge and acronyms.

I am forever changed from the amount I have learnt.

Message to social workers

Thank you.

The amount of work you do behind the scenes is humbling.

I have written before about the hidden work of disasters. I call it the 'bricolage' – there are many spidery threads, which are often not seen by either other responders or survivors, and so much heavy labour that goes into this sort of response. But I see it.

One of the difficulties that we always have with families after a disaster is that they don't know what life might have been like without the social workers. It is so very difficult to measure impact, but please know that the difference you make is life-changing. I honestly do not know what would have happened without you.

Social work managers

Never deploy staff to a disaster setting without training.

This should include specialist training on being present with the families during what is called the *disaster victim identification* process. This process will be run by the police, supporting the family through giving detailed information, medical information and DNA, supporting the family to possibly visit a mortuary and supporting the family all the way through to release of the remains and a funeral. It is important because with so many of our most serious incidents it will be used but so little is known about it. Unfortunately, when it came to Grenfell, there was no time to do anything pre-emptively.

At one level, this was really saddening; however, there was something very organic and authentic about the way people responded, which meant it was from the heart. I also was able to challenge and examine every one of my own guidance documents in a different way than before.

One of the things that really got me was when the social workers that I was working with realised that they were treading a path that many others have walked before. Some of them became quite distressed when they saw the amount of resources that were out there. Families from other large fatal fires who had written testimonies of their experiences raised the same issues that the Grenfell families were feeling. It gave the social workers permission to ask me more and more difficult questions and that felt very necessary.

To illustrate this, many of the families had not been able to see the bodies of their loved ones. Social workers were working through that, not as bereavement counsellors, but by working with people who said they did not believe their loved ones had really gone in the absence of a body. This is a very common reaction to disaster loss but was an area that social workers needed training in. They took a lot of comfort from books like *Collective Conviction* by Anne Eyre and Pamela Dix (2014). This talks in depth about families' experiences of this from other UK disasters.

The social workers were then really upset to realise that was such a common reaction for this kind of sudden disaster. They were very hungry for past experience and knowledge – organisations owe them this, and also owe it to survivors.

I remember running a training day at a point when personal effects had just started to be returned to families. There had been some mistakes and some misunderstanding, but this was a key area of my work, so we basically could run very challenging 'question and answer' sessions. Some social workers challenged me because the families had been offered everything back that could be salvaged, 'even underwear' (the families can, of course, refuse items). There was also distress because the items had 'put people back to the day of the fire'. This is an area where I had lots of videos and personal accounts from other bereaved families who spoke movingly of initially being distressed by items, but over time being able to look at them and process them. We spoke about this at length and arranged for longer storage of the items. Together, the social workers and I lobbied that the families also needed more time for this process, because they were living in hotels so this one box of precious items loomed large in the room and also caused further distress.

Another key message is to keep up-to-date records. There was a huge pressure from central government put on local deliverers to step outside of existing frameworks, and make problems go away. The social workers were in constant fear of being undermined, because they would hold the line on various issues, which would then be overruled by authority. So having accurate records in these contexts is a must.

Be honest with your teams, that this is new to you too. Sometimes the first time that the managers would be able to share was in my training, and then their staff would realise they had no hidden agendas or secret extra resources. They really were in it together.

Finally, and crucially, ensure that staff well-being is prioritised. Annual leave needs to be taken and people need to be allowed to switch off.

After 20 years in the field, I have learnt a fair amount about the importance of self-care, and regularly invest in updates and support around how self-care should be done.

Usually, as a consultant in disaster recovery, the person who looks after me is me. But if needed, I have a trauma debriefer – no one can do this alone, and the same goes for social workers.

Conclusion

The knowledge, skills and understanding gained by social workers in disaster contexts belong not only in their hearts and minds, but in spaces such as these where future practitioners, managers, directors and policy-makers may learn from them. The accounts underscore the value of social work presence in disaster contexts; it is undoubtable that the creativity, insight, compassion, resilience and person-centred practice demonstrated by each contributor would have had a lasting impact on the victim-survivors they supported in ways both tangible and non-tangible. Each extract provides a raw, honest account of the unique challenges social workers can face in disaster contexts, including (but not limited to) the need to balance conflicting risks, the emotional impact of processing traumatic events, cultural differences, and, on a top-down level, a lack of governmental investment, contingency planning, and guidance. A key emerging theme was the way in which systemic inequalities (poverty and racism to name just two) not only increase the likelihood that individuals will face disasters, but also decrease the extent to which they can access effective services. BASW maintains the view that without addressing structural inequalities and austerity, any disaster response will fail to create long-term change.

Reflective questions

- Supervision can be a significant source of professional support. How might this be utilised during a disaster?
- How can employers/organisations offer learning and support and exercise their duty of care in the context of disaster work?

Taking it further

ADASS and BASW (2019) Response and Recommendations from the Task and Finish Groups Looking at: The Role of the DASS and Social Workers in Disaster Recovery. [online] Available at: www.basw.co.uk/system/files/resources/ ADASS%20-%20BASW%20Joint%20Statement%20on%20the%20 role%20of%20SW%20as%20Keyworker.pdf (accessed 11 January 2022).

BASW (nd) *CPD Guidance on Social Work Roles Undertaken during Disasters.* [online] Available at: www.basw.org.uk/system/files/resources/181086%20 CPD%20guidance%20on%20disaster%20social%20work%20V2.pdf (accessed 11 January 2022).

CHAPTER 5

WHO WILL CLAP FOR US? THE ROLE OF SOCIAL WORKERS DURING THE COVID-19 PANDEMIC

In the middle of the most severe global pandemic for many decades, social workers have found themselves working in unfamiliar ways in extraordinary times and having to respond in the midst of unpreparedness, a lack of clarity and confusion. In addition, they are having to adapt to a new form of language, the dictionary of 'coronavirus'. The Coronavirus Act 2020 went through Parliament in less than a week, suspending a range of previous legislation developed over years to support vulnerable children and adults (Legislation. gov.uk, 2020a). While this legislation is exceptional and temporary, it has had a significant impact on the way that social workers practice.

The rights and wrongs of the emergency legislation, regulations and diverse perspectives about parliamentary and judicial democratic processes, scrutiny, and oversight, especially pre- and during lockdown, will not be discussed in detail in this chapter. However, it is important to consider the fast and ever-changing timeline announcements and the political and social environment that social workers were working in at the beginning of the national lockdown. In addition to this, the impact on their own well-being, professional identity and ethical challenges within the context of this disaster will also be explored.

Drawing upon the findings of a British Association of Social Workers (BASW, 2021a) survey (with practitioners during the early stages of the Covid-19 pandemic) this chapter will highlight the personal and professional challenges that social workers juggled daily. A personal reflective case study will be offered by a social worker practising within a hospital setting to bring to life the dilemmas faced by practitioners. The undermining of human rights and the BASW Codes of Ethics will also be considered. The chapter will conclude with key messages to politicians, policy-makers and those who truly want to make a difference.

Self-care

Some readers may find some content distressing. We advise that you take all the time you need when reading, with regular breaks, and reach out for support if needed.

Naming the virus, characterising the pandemic and the dictionary of coronavirus

Covid-19 is an infectious respiratory disease caused by a novel strain of coronavirus (SARS-Cov-2), first detected in Wuhan, China. The name Covid-19 was announced on 11 February 2020 by the World Health Organization (WHO). Director-general Tedros Adhanom Ghebreyesus stated:

> We had to find a name that did not refer to a geographical location, an animal, an individual or group of people, and which is also pronounceable and related to the disease. Having a name matters to prevent the use of other names that can be inaccurate or stigmatizing. It also gives us a standard format to use for any future coronavirus outbreaks.
>
> (WHO, 2020a)

The abbreviation 'Covid' has become a part of everyday language, it is embedded and interwoven into every aspect of our lives, personally and professionally. Social workers have had to reframe their thoughts, actions, practice and terminology in order to adapt their roles to respond to the pandemic. Although the intention to name the virus was not to stigmatise, the reality is that labels including 'Covid', 'coronavirus', 'Covid-19', 'Covid positive', 'asymptomatic', 'underlying health problems', 'shielding' and many more have become part of a new divisive language. This new global language has infiltrated legislation, guidance, policy reform, social work education and practice while creating divisions. It has also provided a framework to deny as well as provide access to resources. The new dictionary of coronavirus continues to dominate social work practice.

During the pandemic, social work students and practitioners have been designated as 'key workers', 'critical workers' and 'essential workers'. The terminology may have been interchangeable, but the critical and essential role of social care and workers has been consistent in government guidance (Department for Education, 2021). Social workers have had to respond in agile ways to a pandemic which has had a multidimensional impact on individuals, families and communities. The virus has had a life-changing global impact on health (physical and mental), social life and the economy. As in other disaster work, Covid-19 has revealed gaps in national pandemic preparedness as well as the role of social workers in such a global emergency (House of Commons, 2021b).

Preparedness – messages to the international community and the introduction of emergency legislation

It is fair to say that social workers alongside other key worker roles in England were not prepared for the pandemic and 'preparedness' was not evident in the constant change of government messages. There were gaps in preparation for a pandemic of this nature and delays in national lockdowns resulting in tragic deaths (House of Commons, 2021b). This resulted in a lack of clarity of social work roles and expectations. Social workers were also managing the unexpected within the context of their personal lives.

To better understand the changing landscape that social workers were operating in, it is important to reflect on some of the statements issued by the WHO and the British government prior to and shortly after the publication of the UK Government and Devolved Administration Coronavirus Action Plan (Department of Health and Social Care, 2020).

Key messages about the importance of local and national preparedness were issued by the WHO including the importance of Covid-19 testing and clinical management (WHO, 2020g). On 15 February 2020 the WHO Director-General, Tedros Adhanom Ghebreyesus, spoke at the Munich Security Conference, International Global Forum, urging the international community to 'use the window of opportunity to intensify preparedness, adopt a whole-of-government *approach and be guided by solidarity, not stigma'*. He also expressed concern at the global lack of *'urgency in funding the response to the pandemic'* (WHO, 2020b). The WHO (2020f) issued guidance for *'preparedness, readiness and response actions for four different transmission scenarios: no cases, sporadic cases, clusters of cases and community transmission'*.

On 3 March 2020, the UK Government and the Devolved Administrations published the *Coronavirus: Action Plan: A Guide to What You Can Expect Across the UK*. The plan highlighted how health and social care systems had *'planned extensively'* for an event like Covid-19 and stated the *'UK is therefore well prepared to respond in a way that offers substantial protection to the public'* (Department of Health and Social Care, 2020).

On 11 March 2020, WHO characterised Covid-19 as a pandemic and continued to express concern at the *'alarming levels of spread and severity, and by the alarming levels of inaction'* (WHO, 2020c).

A recent report has revealed that the UK government did not prepare adequately for the pandemic. Lessons from previous pandemics were not learnt nor did the UK government consider strategies implemented by other countries like China and Italy. This resulted in a delay in the first national lockdown, tragic loss of life especially in care homes and insufficient protective equipment for NHS workers (House of Commons, 2021b). In time, a public inquiry may offer answers to questions about government planning, preparedness, response, learning and impact. *Planning, preparedness, response, learning* and *impact* are all concepts within the disaster cycle; however, there is minimal evidence to support a national and local implementation response to the pandemic (Dominelli, 2014).

We hope that social workers will be called to give evidence at any public inquiry to comment on how health and social care systems had 'planned extensively' for the pandemic.

Changing landscape for social workers

On 12 March 2020, the British Prime Minister Boris Johnson stated: *'I must level with you, level with the British public, many more families are going to lose loved ones before their time'* (UK Government, 2020a). It is worth noting that this attitude of succumbing to disaster and accepting the inevitability of mass deaths contrasted with that of Jacinda Ardern, prime minister of New Zealand, who, on 23 March 2020, said:

> *The worst-case scenario is simply intolerable. It would represent the greatest loss of New Zealanders' lives in our country's history. I will not take that chance. The government will do all it can to protect you. None of us can do this alone.*

(Roy, 2020)

In a further announcement a few days later, Boris Johnson, speaking more optimistically, told the nation about *'our overall plan for beating this new coronavirus... we know how to beat it and we know that if as a country we follow the scientific advice that is now being given we know that we will beat it'* (UK Government, 2020b). Social workers were hearing these government announcements at the same time as other citizens, trying to digest and understand what was being shared, uncertain of their roles and what support could be offered safely to the children, families and adults they worked with.

On 19 March 2020, the Department for Health and Social Care and Public Health England published an ethical framework for adult social care, a framework to support the planning and organisation of adult social care during the coronavirus. Excluding this framework there was no other bespoke Public Health England or other government policy guidance specifically for social workers issued in England at this time.

Following the announcement of the nationwide lockdown on 23 March 2020, the public were advised they could only shop for necessities, leave their homes for exercise once a day or for any medical need or to provide care or to help a vulnerable person, and to work from home unless it was necessary to travel to and from work (UK Government, 2020c).

On 25 March 2020, emergency legislation received Royal assent and the Coronavirus Act 2020 was passed covering England, Wales, Scotland, and Northern Ireland (Legislation.gov.uk, 2020a).

Not only were social workers (alongside other key workers and citizens) having to live and work in the context of a nationwide lockdown, initially with little (if any) access to personal protective equipment (PPE) but they were also working in a changing landscape of emergency legislation, with no operating social care guidance or processes at a local or national level. This changed over time, but social workers reported the following (BASW, 2020a).

> 'Social workers are being asked to buy washing up bowls to keep in their car and wash their hands in between visits.'

> 'I'm pregnant and despite being in one of the most vulnerable groups I am still being told it would be a choice to self-isolate. In other words, if I don't turn up, I won't be paid.'

> 'Lack of resources for keeping ourselves and the public safe. All we've been given are some tubes of wipes for the room. No hand sanitisers to be seen and the cleaning of door handles/lifts hasn't been upped. We are looking after ourselves, bringing in cleaning products to clean down desks and phones.'

> 'We are being told business as usual. Keep visuals to a bare minimum and doing a lot on the phones. However, we have NO personal protective equipment, no hand sanitiser or aprons or masks available.'

A disaster was unfolding, and social workers were not physically equipped, nor aware of how the announcement of temporary legislation would restrict their roles and redefine access to support and resources for children, families and adults.

Temporary legislative measures

Social workers were constantly having to adapt to, and understand, emerging new powers, temporary emergency legislation, regulations and a raft of public health and NHS guidance that had consequences for the individuals and the communities they serve.

The Care Act 2014 first came into effect in 2015. The stated purpose of adult care and support is to help people to achieve the outcomes that matter to them in their life. An important principle of the Care Act is supporting people to participate as fully as possible in decisions about their care and support.

The Coronavirus Act 2020 enabled the government to introduce temporary changes called 'easements to legislation' including the Care Act 2014. These 'easements' came into force on 31 March 2020 and made it possible for local authorities to no longer provide detailed assessments of people's care and support needs if they were unable to meet their full duties in accordance with the temporary powers because of acute staff shortages or high demand.

Ethical challenges, erosion of legal and human rights and the emerging conflict of the role for social workers in this disaster began to escalate.

Throughout the pandemic, individuals and human rights organisations such as Amnesty International UK and Article 39 and charities such as Mencap and advocacy groups have consistently raised concerns about the application of emergency legislation (Amnesty International, 2020; Willow, 2020; Mencap, 2021). This has included the Care Act easement guidance and The Adoption and Children (Coronavirus) (Amendments) Regulations 2020, that temporarily amended ten sets of regulations relating to children's social care (Legislation.gov.uk, 2020b).

There were legal challenges to emergency legislation and regulations and following an appeal brought by Article 39 the High Court found that the 'Secretary of State acted unlawfully by failing to consult the Children's Commissioner and other bodies representing the rights of children in care before introducing The Adoption and Children (Coronavirus) (Amendment) (No1) Regulations 2020' (Willow, 2020). This challenge resulted in The Adoption and Children (Coronavirus) (Amendment) (No 2) Regulations 2020 being extended until 31 September 2020 and removed the majority of the original amendments (House of Commons, 2021a).

New and emerging legislation and regulation provided a legal framework for social workers to diversify their practice when undertaking their work with adults, children and families, including, for example, allowing visits to take place over the telephone or via a video link or other electronic communication methods when it was not possible to undertake a face-to-face visit (UK Parliament, 2021).

Public Health England and the government-issued guidance throughout 2020 and 2021 recommended and then formalised a ban on visits to care homes by family, friends and next of kin. Emergency legislation was introduced without public consultation and as time progressed following the initial national lockdown and subsequent national restrictions increasing, voices of opposition were raised about ethical and human rights issues including the blanket ban approach of no visits to care homes and an emerging horror at the non-consensual approach to 'Do not resuscitate'.

Mencap reported receiving information from people with learning disabilities that they had been told they would not be resuscitated if they were taken ill with Covid-19 (Mencap, 2021). The Care Quality Commission reported that the blanket and inappropriate use of 'Do not attempt cardiopulmonary resuscitation' (DNACPR) potentially caused avoidable deaths (Care Quality Commission, 2020).

Covid-19 – a threat to human rights and ethical values

The International Federation of Social Work (IFSW) and International Association of Schools of Social Work (IASSW) global definition of social work states:

> *Social work is a practice-based profession and an academic discipline that promotes social change and development, social cohesion, and the empowerment and liberation of people. Principles of social justice, human rights, collective responsibility, and respect for diversities are central to social work. Underpinned by theories of social work, social sciences, humanities and indigenous knowledge, social work engages people and structures to address life challenges and enhance well-being. The above definition may be amplified at national and/or regional levels.*

(IFSW, 2014)

The Professional Capabilities Framework (PCF) is the framework for social work learning and practice in England (BASW, 2018). The 2018 refresh sets out nine common domains of capability and promotes social work as 'one profession'. All of the domains sit within three overarching super domains, *purpose, practice* and *impact*.

Professional Capabilities Framework

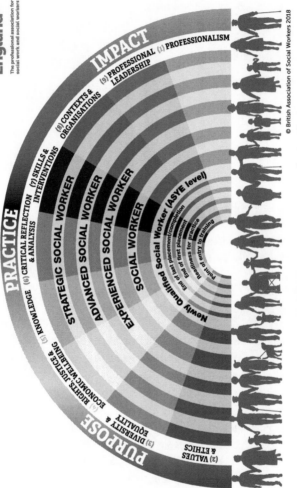

www.basw.co.uk/pcf

● The PCF nine domains:

- values and ethics;
- diversity and equality;
- rights, justice and economic well-being;
- knowledge;
- critical reflection and analysis;
- skills and interventions;
- context and organisations;
- leadership;
- professionalism.

The PCF, together with the IFSW/IASSW definition of social work and the BASW Code of Ethics have a symbiotic relationship, reinforcing social work values, ethics, professional capabilities, expectations of social workers and the unity and strength of 'one global profession'. Capabilities are *'An integration of knowledge, skills, personal qualities, behaviour, understanding, and values used appropriately, effectively and confidently, not just in familiar and highly focused specialist contexts but in response to new, complex and changing circumstances'* (Stephenson and Weil, 1992; BASW, 2018).

Social work is a human rights-based profession, founded upon values and principles of social justice and equality. Never has it been more important to grasp tightly onto sound ethics and values as it has been during the Covid-19 pandemic, as inequalities and threats to human rights have been exposed. This in part is due to the growing pressures put upon individuals and families already experiencing social and financial hardship at a time when local services have been under significant strain due to austerity measures. As stated by BASW on the role of social workers in a pandemic and its aftermath: *'The starkest expression of this is in the inequality of access to protection from abuse and neglect, access to treatment to sustain life, and the unequal and devastating death rates in our society'* (BASW, 2020b).

Advocating for human rights is a core professional value and resonates with calls for social justice from previous disasters in England, including the

Hillsborough football tragedy and Grenfell Tower fire in London. The BASW Code of Ethics (BASW, 2021b) promotes the professional values, principles and ethics on which the profession is based including:

- recognising diversity;
- upholding and promoting human dignity and well-being;
- promoting the right to self-determination and participation;
- challenging discrimination;
- treating each person as a whole;
- upholding the values and reputation of the profession; and
- developing professional relationships and challenging the abuse of human rights.

The Code of Ethics highlights the importance of social workers applying their professional obligations in the diverse roles and responsibilities they fulfil.

During the pandemic social workers have had to deal with many ethical challenges. This included the application of emergency legislation and guidance, rationing resources and support, discharge to assess for people leaving hospital care (see case study). Also, not seeing people they work with face to face, advocating for best interests and promoting the importance of informed consent in a context of closed cultures following government directives, for example, for people to stay at home.

Social workers have shared the ethical and professional challenges of practising in a pandemic, particularly in relation to safeguarding and accessing those they support within the community. They have also had to adapt to flexible models of working while endeavouring to uphold professional social work relationships and maintaining their statutory responsibilities.

According to a BASW survey on the impact of Covid-19 on the profession, 63.5 per cent of respondents agreed or strongly agreed that they had encountered more ethical and moral dilemmas since the introduction of lockdown restrictions (BASW, 2021a). Furthermore, 51.5 per cent of respondents agreed or strongly agreed that they had encountered more difficulties in monitoring safeguarding access/carrying out safe and effective adult and child protection visits because of limited face-to-face access (BASW, 2021a). Social workers have had to juggle all of this, in addition to dealing with personal and professional challenges and inequalities and working within an unknown context. The pandemic has tested and continues to test the professional confidence, capabilities, skills and expertise of social workers. Like other professionals, social workers have had to work with risk, ambiguity, complexity and uncertainty. More than ever, in their professional and personal lives, they have had to draw upon and apply their transferable knowledge, theory and practice to the new world of living and working during a pandemic.

Ethical challenges – working within a context of social injustice

As highlighted by the voices of people with lived experience and social workers in this book, the impact of a disaster and the response to it will magnify inequalities and social injustice. Despite the efforts of naming the pandemic Covid-19 to avoid discrimination, the pandemic has reinforced and fuelled the ugly and cruel nature of discrimination. This is described as the 'targeting of the other' on a global scale. In this context, the 'other' refers to *the foreigner or someone belonging to ethnic or cultural minority groups*' (UNESCO, 2020).

During the first phase of the pandemic, blame was erroneously focused upon those who were considered as the cause of the disease, for example Asian people and those of Asian descent. This included reports of acts of discrimination consisting of verbal abuse in public places, demeaning social media campaigns, boycotts of businesses and in some cases a denial of access to educational establishments (UNESCO, 2020).

A report by Amnesty International exposed the disproportionate targeting by police across Europe of ethnic minority and marginalised groups with identity checks, forced quarantines and fines. Forms of discrimination overflowed into other groups and towards Roma communities and asylum seekers living in shared accommodation (Amnesty International, 2020; UNESCO, 2020).

The Covid-19 pandemic has amplified the social disparities that already exist in society. This can be seen in the ways it has disproportionately affected Black, Asian and minority ethnic communities, older people, households on low income, women, children and those with disabilities to name but a few intersectionalities.

A report produced by Public Health England (2020) found that certain factors mean that individuals are more likely to get seriously ill or not recover from coronavirus. These include: age (increases as you get older), living in poor geographical areas, being from a Black, Asian or minority ethnic background, and being born outside of the UK or Ireland. Living in a care home and certain jobs such as nurses, taxi drivers and security guards add to the risk. Gender is also a factor, as men are more likely to become seriously unwell or die from Covid-19 once it is contracted (Powles, 2020).

A recent survey revealed that most social workers in England believe that the Covid-19 pandemic has greatly reduced the capacity of their service and that people they support have been adversely affected (Turner, 2020). Social workers responding to the survey warned of *'compounding hardships'*, where adults with mental health issues were being forced to stay at home, with services suspended or greatly reduced. Similarly, adults with learning difficulties experienced a loss of routine and activity during lockdown which in turn increased levels of anxiety, especially for those with autism. Indeed, analysis by Mencap revealed Covid-19-related deaths of those with a learning disability were dramatically higher than the general population in England and Wales, with up to 45 per cent being Covid-19 related (Mencap, 2021). The analysis cited previous data from Public Health England (2020), which showed that people with a learning disability in England were dying from Covid-19 at six times the rate of the general population between 21 March and 5 June 2020.

Older people

Covid-19 has had a particularly harsh impact on older people, especially those living in care homes. Between the week ending 20 March 2020 and the week ending 2 April 2021, 24.3 per cent of all registered deaths in care homes (totalling 42,341) were Covid-19 related (Office for National Statistics, 2021). A recent report states:

> The lack of priority attached to social care during the initial phase of the pandemic was illustrative of a longstanding failure to afford social care the same attention as the NHS. The rapid discharge of people from hospitals into care homes without adequate testing or rigorous isolation was indicative of the disparity. It is understandable that the Government should move quickly to avoid hospitals being overwhelmed but it was a

mistake to allow patients to be transferred to care homes without the rigour shown in places like Germany and Hong Kong. This, combined with untested staff bringing infection into homes from the community, led to many thousands of deaths which could have been avoided.

(House of Commons, 2021b, p 8)

The horrors of what unfolded with older patients being discharged from hospital, many without being tested for Covid-19, and returned to live in care homes or placed in care homes for the first time, had a devastating impact for individuals, families, care staff and allied professionals, including social workers. The loss of life and impact on loved ones and the bereaved has been painful and significant.

Closed communities emerged, family members could not visit loved ones in care homes and social workers faced ethical challenges of not undertaking direct contact and visits and feeling compromised about their ability to safeguard adults and children.

Children and young people

Social workers working in children's services expressed similar concerns with worries about the impact of lockdown on children's education, rising levels of domestic abuse and the increase in poverty (Turner, 2020). From the onset of the lockdown restrictions, there have been concerns regarding rising incidents of domestic abuse. The National Domestic Abuse helpline witnessed a 25 per cent increase in calls and online requests for help, warning that the restrictions heighten domestic tension and serve to further entrap women and their children in abusive households (Townsend, 2020).

Research by the NSPCC has identified that social isolation has increased the risk of child abuse during and after the Covid-19 pandemic. The study confirms that the risk of abuse to children is higher when parents and carers are more stressed due to the challenges that the pandemic has caused. It also highlights that children and young people are more vulnerable to certain types of abuse such as online, within the home, criminal activity and child sexual exploitation. This is exacerbated with the reduction of normal protective services such as schools and other social connections (Romanou and Belton, 2020).

National youth homelessness helplines have reported a doubling in calls during the Covid-19 lockdown, many from young people trapped in abusive households. This was compounded by the withdrawal of the limited support services and the shortage of suitable accommodation options. On 26 March 2020, the Minister for Rough Sleeping and Housing, Luke Hall MP, in a letter to local authority leaders, announced the 'Everyone in' policy (Hall, 2020). It is estimated that because of this policy, almost 15,000 rough sleepers were placed in hotels or emergency accommodation. The government created a specific budget for local authorities to help them manage the process. The 'Everyone in' policy highlights how rough sleeping can be eliminated when there is political will, commitment and resources available (Wirral Ark, 2020). However, some argue that the policy name is misleading as the government did not clarify the parameters of the policy until some weeks after the announcement explaining that 'Everyone in' was only intended to cover individuals identified as homeless pre-lockdown – not those made homeless during lockdown. By this time, local authorities had allocated resources. As Andy Burnham, mayor of Greater Manchester, argued in a letter to the secretary of state: *'Calling this policy "Everyone in" at the start only to define what that means later down the line has unfairly left councils facing unfunded costs'* (Burnham, 2020).

Conflicts of interest – the personal and professional experiences of social workers

Social workers are experienced in working within a context of uncertainty, adopting a strengths-based approach, and managing risk; however, never have social workers in the UK worked and lived in a pandemic – and they continue to do so. The daily experiences of life with Covid-19 have impacted upon everyone, from queuing for food and necessary items at the beginning of the pandemic to social distancing, wearing PPE and not being allowed to mix with others, which in turn has created a sense of severe isolation and closed communities. Social workers have continued to visit children, families, and vulnerable adults whenever possible. However, the 'office' environment has physically and emotionally invaded people's homes and their personal lives. Work–life balance has become blurred and digital platforms and social media have become the increasing norm for communication.

Social workers have shared their experiences about the initial challenges of accessing PPE (BASW, 2021a), confusion about local and national guidance, fears about not seeing the people they work with, safeguarding in relation to children and adults, and not being able to adhere to guidance and regulations (BASW, 2021a). The constant change of the 'rules' in addition to dealing with ethical conflicts has created moral distress for social workers.

The emerging themes from the BASW survey (2021a) include:

- issues surrounding access to, use of and storage of personal protective equipment;
- regional variation and confusion about national guidance from both government and Public Health England;
- difficulty in keeping up with new guidance being issued; and
- fear of the unknown, new ways of working and increased use of electronic communication and digital platforms.

This was all underpinned by concerns about transmitting or catching Covid-19. Worries about children, young people, adults and carers both in the work context and in personal life centred around ethical dilemmas, social injustice and inequalities.

Much of the data gathered in the survey illustrates the unimaginable hardship faced by social workers during the pandemic, something which though hard-hitting, can seem far-off in the absence of stories. The following case study brings some of these challenges to life. It is offered by a social worker who we have not named due to the sensitive issues raised by their story and offers a unique insight into the realities of working within the context of a hospital and having responsibility for discharging patients during a global pandemic.

Case study

How the pandemic impacted hospital social work

Like many social workers, I wear several hats. I am a hospital social worker as part of a discharge social work team, as well as a practice educator and teacher.

During the coronavirus I was working as part of a hospital discharge team, which gave me unique insight into the challenges faced by frontline staff across both health and social care.

Under normal circumstances, my role involves assessing patients and engaging with families. This therapeutic way of working stopped during the pandemic and was replaced by a Covid-19 discharge process which removed social workers from wards. Our role became following up with patients 24 hours after leaving hospital, as part of a team of professionals. This involved ensuring an individual package of care was met under a 'discharge to assess pathway' – something patients are eligible for if they have significant health needs.

Use of PPE

For any social worker, wearing PPE and observing social distancing was/is challenging. But for hospital social workers there is an additional layer of complexity. Our role is more fluid and changes from assessor to commissioner or care provider. For example, if I found a discharged patient soiled or incontinent, I could not leave the patient until they were attended to, and the two-metre distance rule becomes theoretical. These concerns could have been lessened if we were given the same support as colleagues on wards. However, from my experience, we lacked the same level of PPE, changing facilities or access points to wash after visits. Disposing of PPE in and of itself was also a risk, as was the possibility of carrying the Covid-19 virus on personal clothing during visits. We were agents of help but also potentially vessels of the virus.

Legislative changes

A shift away from the Care Act 2014 legal framework meant social workers were not receiving admission notifications. This requires hospitals to notify Adult Social Care of the likelihood of a patient's

→

need for community care services. Nor were we receiving estimated date of discharge notifications. As a result, social workers relied on overworked hospital staff to discharge patients. This way of working risked patients being discharged to various settings without the knowledge of social work teams. It highlighted how integral our role is, and consequences that occur when our support is not available.

Home working

Maintaining confidentiality was a significant challenge for social workers during lockdown and working at home. Overnight, our homes became offices as well as family/communal spaces. More consideration is needed where home environments become an 'office' environment when carrying out a professional role. Less talked-about issues include an increase in bills for maintaining a home office, which were not compensated for. This has put a financial strain on professionals who were already facing competing challenges.

Personal responsibilities

For social workers with children or caring responsibilities, home working can be a particular challenge. Young children may be left on their own without stimulation, which could leave them feeling neglected and the parent/carer feeling guilty. The pandemic posed a difficult balancing act for social workers who had high levels of demand at both home and work.

What support is needed in future emergencies?

- *Practical support:* Access to functioning IT systems and PPE should be standard. There should be no hierarchies between which professional has access to the highest quality equipment based on their role or setting.

- *Psychosocial support:* Access to psychosocial support could help practitioners see things from a different perspective. Supporting social workers' well-being should be a priority, as it helps to build on resilience which will lead to better capacity to carry out required tasks (WHO, 2020d).

- *Enhanced connection, the right environment and relationship-based practice:* It is important for practitioners to keep connected with colleagues to maintain a sense of belonging and promote team morale. This reflects a relationship-based approach which is critical to keep the team moving forward and focused. The focus on a relationship-based approach centres around showing empathy, neutrality/objectivity and trust and being supportive of each other (Ruch et al, 2010). Teams need access to an environment where they can offload so they do not become emotionally bogged down, lonely, or undervalued. Regular debriefing is essential to ensure workers feel ready, safe, and well. If contact is poor, workers may feel disconnected, isolated, or abandoned. Relationship-based practice must be at the heart of future responses.

The above case study highlights the British government's mishandling of PPE during the first wave of the Covid-19 pandemic. This is confirmed in a report which states that health and social care colleagues experienced a shortage of PPE even in high-risk settings like hospitals and care homes for older people (House of Commons, 2021b). It also indicates the implications of changes to legislative frameworks, the impact of home working, the burden of juggling personal caring responsibilities and the need for support on both a practical and emotional level. The importance of relationship-based practice remains core to social work practice.

Disaster cycle

Social workers have a long history of responding to critical incidents and disasters in England and play an integral role in prevention, immediate relief, recovery, reconstruction and promoting self-care. Their professional ethics, values, knowledge and skills are all essential requisites in an emergency (ADASS and BASW, 2019).

The experiences of social workers during the pandemic have mirrored different stages in the disaster cycle, and some of the ethical dilemmas faced by social workers in helping those bereaved, victims and survivors of other disasters. Social workers are often the unsung responders not recognised pre-, during and post-disaster and this has been increasingly evident during the pandemic. Government sound bites of *protect the NHS* have put the important role of health workers in the spotlight; however, the recognition of the pivotal role and contribution of social workers has been minimal in comparison.

As Dominelli (2014, p 4) states:

> Social workers are usually found offering practical assistance on the ground, rather than occupying the media spotlight. Their endeavours and contributions are rarely highlighted as social work interventions, and so the people social workers engage with specifically are usually the ones aware of their activities.

As stated earlier in this chapter, it is questionable if the UK government mitigated and minimised the effects of the pandemic, or were prepared and able to respond to minimise the risks. It may be argued that we are still not in the recovery stage of the pandemic, and this will be a long journey, with sporadic stages of the disaster cycle being replayed (Dominelli, 2014).

At the onset of the first national lockdown in England, social workers were reporting a lack of mitigation, prevention and preparedness by organisations and government. There was a void of local policy and practice guidance in response to the pandemic, with reported shortages of PPE and shortage of essential supplies in some shops. Home working became the default, virtual relationship-based social work the norm and practitioners reported challenges with fragile IT and business support systems and human resources. Some reported IT systems crashing due to increased use of digital technology. Professional in-person contact with peers, and work-based contact with children, families and adults was not encouraged and if it did take place, two metres social distancing had to be adhered to. Direct face-to-face contact with social workers became the exception rather than the norm, excluding adherence to statutory functions and risks being assessed.

For all these challenges social workers did what they do best: they have adapted, been responsive as a profession, diversified and become innovators of change during the pandemic.

Ruth Allen (2020), the chief executive officer (CEO) for BASW, suggests that the Covid-19 pandemic will transform social work in the UK. Public support for the profession will increase as referrals to public services surge following lockdown revealing both the social need and social work's role in responding and meeting this need. Covid-19 has revealed itself as a psychosocial crisis as well as a public health emergency which might bring mental health practice and social work closer together. Allen (2020) goes on to conclude that while social workers, like many other professionals, will adapt to a *new normal*, there is the potential for their working conditions to improve with the introduction of more readily available self-care resources, meaningful flexible working, and personalised risk assessments.

Conclusion

The unique contribution and pivotal role of social workers in past disasters, during the pandemic, its aftermath and subsequent recovery, should be recognised at a political and national leadership level. Social workers are integral to supporting citizens and local communities and working in partnership with stakeholders at a local 'place' level, in mobilising and supporting a strengths-based community development approach.

Social workers must be supported and empowered to contribute, shape, influence and access disaster training and continuous professional development (CPD). Social workers and people with lived experience have developed the BASW England CPD guidance which focuses on core areas of leadership and practice: learning and development, knowledge and understanding, evaluation and analysis, and skills and application. It is important that employers and organisations prioritise well-being and aspects of practice that are highlighted. These include the diverse perspectives of those who have been affected or impacted by disasters, and, reflecting on the wider contexts, causes and implications of disasters.

The guidance is mapped against the Professional Capabilities Framework and the Knowledge and Skills Statements. It is envisaged that this guidance will be a small but significant initial step towards a nationally co-ordinated and consistent approach to the training and development of social workers.

The pandemic has touched the lives and practice of all social workers in England. Everyone has had to adapt to national and regional lockdowns, new ways of working, supporting people in and outside of work, work–life demands and pressures, and local place response systems. As a profession, social workers deserve to be recognised for their extraordinary contribution during this pandemic and other disasters.

A bright light needs to be shone on this amazing profession. Social workers need to be supported to come out of the shadows, be valued and recognised for their contributions during disasters, past and present, in the recovery phase of the pandemic and in preparing for the future. Social workers really do make a difference. Margaret Aspinall, who shares her experiences of the Hillsborough disaster in Chapter 3, said of her social worker: *'Antoinette saved my life.'*

Reflective questions

- What does the international definition of social work mean to you in the context of your practice in the current political climate?
- How have you shared your experiences of working within a pandemic with your peers, supervisor and organisation?

Taking it further

BASW (2020, 28 May) The Role of Social Workers in a Pandemic and its Aftermath: Learning from Covid-19. [online] Available at: www.basw.co.uk/role-social-workers-pandemic-and-its-aftermath-learning-covid-19 (accessed 11 January 2022).

BASW (2021, 28 January) Social Work during the Covid-19 Pandemic: Initial Findings. [online] Available at: www.basw.co.uk/resources/social-work-during-covid-19-pandemic-initial-findings (accessed 11 January 2022).

House of Commons (2021, 12 October) Coronavirus: Lessons Learned to Date. Sixth Report of the Health and Social Care Committee and Third Report of the Science and Technology Committee of Session 2021–22. [online] Available at: https://committees.parliament.uk/publications/7496/documents/78687/default/ (accessed 11 January 2022).

Statement given to BASW by Covid Families for Justice

The UK Government's actions have led to the highest death toll in Europe. But this isn't about statistics. Every single one of the tens of thousands of deaths from Covid-19 recorded in the UK represents a living, breathing person, taken before their time. We can't let this keep on happening. But we family members, and the country, deserve answers.

CHAPTER 6

LEARNING
FOR THE FUTURE

This final chapter draws together the learning from the rich stories of those with lived experience, practitioners and their leaders. It will focus on significant learning points from these perspectives and highlight some areas of good practice to emulate. Links are made to the challenge of working ethically at a time when the nature of crises involved fast-paced, often scary work, with little time for reflection. Reflection on what we have learnt from these disasters about the impact on individuals, communities and professionals will also be considered. It also considers the impact of the media in its varied forms in times of disasters and reflects on the many occasions in the past where social work contributions have been overlooked. The significance of the role of social work within disasters embedded within a professional learning process will be supported by the BASW guidance as a recommended educational component in the preparation for disaster work.

Self-care

Some readers may find some content distressing. We advise that you take all the time you need when reading, with regular breaks, and reach out for support if needed.

Impact of disasters on social workers

There is a shared understanding that professionals, including social workers and volunteers, exposed to disasters and who engage in work with traumatised people and communities, are likely to experience their own trauma. There is a considerable amount of literature which focuses on the psychological impact of disasters on 'helping professionals' who provide assistance and support to victims and survivors. These include an array of negative and positive effects. The negative effects include symptoms associated with post-traumatic stress disorders (PTSD) such as grief, loss, fear, uncertainty and a sense of helplessness which are connected with the professionals' exposure to the disaster (Baum, 2014). Other effects include vicarious trauma which is described as the *'process of change resulting from empathetic engagement with trauma survivors'* (BMA, 2020). This is typically manifested in feelings of anger, sadness, guilt, detachment, pessimism, overly emotional involvement or over-identification with victims and survivors leading to difficulties in maintaining professional boundaries. The damaging effects can be cumulative and pervasive and vary from individual to individual (Michalopoulos and Aparicio, 2012).

There are also times when the social worker might belong to the same community or geographical area and so is exposed to the same common disaster. This is referred to as a *'shared traumatic reality'* or *'double exposure'* (Baum, 2014, p 2113). This is particularly relevant in the stories shared in this book by colleagues who live and work around the Manchester Arena and Grenfell Tower areas, and during the Covid-19 pandemic.

It has been suggested that those involved in working in disasters experience an impact on three levels: personal, professional and ethical (Cooper et al, 2018). The 'personal' relates to the actual or perceived risk to one's own life and the exposure to the sights and stories of death, suffering, loss and disruption. 'Professional' impacts are associated with the disruption of infrastructures, policy and routine mandatory expectations such as case recording and supervision. Working in disasters frequently provokes complex dilemmas and decision-making often connected with the allocation of resources and time which can present challenges to practitioners' ethical values (Cooper et al, 2018).

Much has been written about grief and bereavement and well-known cycles have been developed in an endeavour to make sense of the experience of loss. The Trauma and Stress Disorder Working Group of the World Health Organization (WHO) has proposed the inclusion of a new condition of prolonged grief disorder (ICD-11). They outline a list of examples of emotional pain which includes sadness, guilt and difficulty in accepting the death. It is also sometimes referred to as complicated grief or unresolved or traumatic grief which is highly relevant in the context of social work in disasters and tragic events (Mauro et al, 2019).

Healing together

In keeping with a strengths-based approach, the concept of post-traumatic growth introduces the idea of looking beyond the negative effects of disaster on the lives of people, which Tudor et al (2015) argue has traditionally been the focus of disaster recovery. Post-traumatic growth is a term that is often used interchangeably with vicarious resilience, where individuals experience a positive transformation and a sense of empowerment as a result of engaging with victims and survivors (Quitangon and Evces, 2015). Post-traumatic growth refers to the positive psychological shift experienced because of adversity which can lead to a change in perspective, potentially leading to meaningful personal growth. One of the defining characteristics of a disaster is the social context in which it occurs.

'Survivors experience disasters, subsequent loss and grief in a community context, and the validation received through social support is important to the resolution of grief' (Beinecke et al, 2017, p 94). Tragic events can unite people through community, family, work, geography, personal characteristics (such as race, gender, national identification) and so the significance of collective and advocacy-based support becomes even more meaningful. Typically, in the immediate aftermath of a disaster, support and/or campaigning groups are formed in solidarity to consider the short- and long-term implications of experiencing a disaster. Examples of this include Grenfell United, Hillsborough Family Support Group, Hillsborough Justice Campaign, and Hope for Hillsborough. Inevitably, the road to recovery and healing can be lonely and collective rituals can offer some comfort. These rituals take on many forms and range from artwork, memorials that keep the memory of those who lost their lives alive, or the power of silence as was witnessed in the silent walks held by the Grenfell Tower survivors, community and supporters.

Other than the experience of surviving a disaster itself, the thing that can gather strangers in unity is the shared commonality that brought them to the event in the first place. Survivors then use this common interest to draw strength from one another; this may be, for instance, a love of music or sport. Examples of this include the 4.15 Strong running group, set up by survivors of the Boston, USA, terrorist bombing in 2013 (4.15 refers to the date of the bombing). Closer to home, the Manchester Survivors Choir was set up by social worker Cath Hill, who attended the Ariana Grande concert with her ten-year-old son. As well as the experience changing Cath and her family's approach to life and safety, using her social work knowledge, she set up a peer-to-peer support group in the form of a choir for those affected by the bombing. In Cath's words:

> So, why a choir? Those of us who were registered victims of the attacks were added to an online forum... On that, we recognised that we all had something in common (other than the huge thing we had in common of course), which was that our kids loved music. That's why they were at the arena that night. People were posting about their kids struggling to engage in singing and dancing as they had done before the attacks and through discussion it was suggested that maybe we should start our own choir.
>
> (BASW, nd)

For those social workers who have been involved in a disaster in a professional capacity, supervision plays a significant role in reducing the impact of vicarious trauma (Joubert et al, 2013; Michalopoulos and Aparicio, 2012). Self-care for social workers is an integral aspect of professionalism and is intricately linked to our ability to provide the best possible service to those we work with and for. As a response to the recent global pandemic, BASW produced a quick guide for social workers to promote and prioritise self-care. Arguably, the principles of this guide are relevant to all practitioners involved in disasters work, and it stresses the importance of providing and receiving supervision (BASW, 2020a). For individuals, BASW (2020a) encourages:

- self-awareness to monitor our own well-being;

- taking appropriate leave when necessary;

- maintaining a personal routine which includes hobbies and exercise;

- developing a flexible approach;

- ensuring there is clarity around the remit of our role;

- identifying a professional and personal support system;

- seeking support when necessary;

- taking time to reflect;

- asking questions to provide clarification;

- limiting exposure to news updates and social media posts;

- seeking out debriefing sessions and supervision; and

- using humour appropriately.

As healing happens on a collective as well as an individual level, BASW (2020a) suggests that teams:

- remain supportive;

- develop a buddy system;

- provide debriefing sessions;

- engage in supervision;

- reach out to team members;

- provide email communication and information in a manageable way;

- ensure colleagues know where to gain necessary support;

- require and encourage colleagues to take leave and breaks; and

- provide support for home working where necessary.

Recovery is not time-limited

Living through a global pandemic has highlighted that social workers, like so many others, were working with loss while experiencing personal losses of their own. The abrupt and unexpected end of life, with people not being able to say goodbye in person or at all, is a common theme in messages of people who have survived a disaster. The theory of applying a strengths-based approach to trauma-informed practice and the stark reality of living and working in a context of trauma and experiencing vicarious trauma cannot be underestimated. What happens when the physical, psychological and emotional safety of all parts of the community of social work are impacted? Who supports the workforce to reclaim control of their professional and personal lives when they themselves are tired, traumatised and bereaved, while endeavouring to support others on a daily basis?

In the months and years following a disaster, BASW has heard that social workers and survivors are still sharing their experiences about guilt and what they have and have not been able to do for their families, friends and the people they work with. This is often described as *survivor guilt*, which relates to a sense of guilt for surviving or being uninjured when others were or being unable to do more for the victims of the disaster.

Theoretical models are useful to inform disaster and social work practice. However, we also need to recognise that the unique lived experience of individuals and communities does not neatly fit into a particular timely stage of disaster recovery – it is not time-limited. We know from the voices of those living with the experience in this book, that for some there is no recovery – you learn to live with a situation, you do not recover from it. There is a strong message from brave contributors in this book about the importance of social workers understanding that recovery is not a fixed concept, it is not time-limited. Disasters are horrific and the legacy lives on for generations and, as we have seen, in many instances so does the battle for social justice. Social workers have an important role to play in advocating and promoting social justice for others and themselves.

Trauma-informed practice

The challenges faced by a traumatised workforce who are working with and supporting people who themselves have been traumatised cannot be underestimated. Trauma-informed practice is a strengths-based model which is rooted in an *'understanding of and responsiveness to the impact of trauma, that emphasizes physical, psychological, and emotional safety for both providers and survivors, and that creates opportunities for survivors to rebuild a sense of control and empowerment'* (Hopper et al, 2010).

● It is important to note that, similar to disasters, resulting trauma does not discriminate across intersectionalities – it has no boundaries with regard to *'age, gender, socioeconomic status, race, ethnicity, geography or sexual orientation'* (SAMHSA, 2014). The majority of people will experience at least one traumatic event in their lifetime.

Within the context of a global pandemic, social workers have had to manage the personal and professional impact of national lockdowns, separation from loved ones, isolation, remote working, minimising in-person contact with other human beings – the very core of relationship-based social work. The psychological impact of dealing with the 'unknown', the fear of contracting Covid-19, the responsibility of maintaining the safety and well-being of self and others, the isolation of remote working and the slow burn of fatigue have all taken their toll.

Theoretical models can create useful frameworks to explore how survivors of disasters rebuild their lives, regain personal control and empower themselves. However, the messages from people with lived experience in this book have highlighted that there is no 'one size fits all' model. Each individual, family and community finds, or at least attempts to find, their own way to live with the unbearable.

Post-traumatic stress disorder

Post-traumatic stress disorder (PTSD) is a potential diagnosis in anyone who has experienced or witnessed a traumatic event or multiple events; there is no timeline within which such events must have happened, and they can be located many years in the past or recently (NICE, 2018). The symptoms of PTSD can be wide-ranging, and include, but are not limited to, reliving the traumatic event through nightmares and flashbacks, feelings of isolation, irritability and guilt, and difficulties in sleeping and concentrating (NHS, 2018).

Social workers play a pivotal role in responding to disasters, as highlighted in this book, and have been providing 24/7 services throughout the pandemic. Some will have directly experienced traumatic events and others may have experienced vicarious trauma. Many will have worked long hours, without the ability to take breaks or, due to lack of support, maintain their well-being, leading to both fatigue and burnout.

Disasters are not neatly packaged events with a clear beginning, middle and end. Nor do they occur in sterile, contained environments. Rather, they are messy, painful and in many instances physically horrific (Myers and Wee, 2005). A disaster environment may consist of *difficult emotional conditions, exposure to gruesome sites, sickening odors, danger, destruction of physical surroundings and social order breakdown* (Naturale, 2007, p 174).

That social workers are disproportionately impacted by PTSD is well established, with both clinical observations and empirical reports showing that indirect exposure to traumatic material is associated with high rates of post-traumatic stress disorder symptoms among social workers (Bride, 2007). Furthermore, listening to trauma narratives also can increase the risk of vicarious traumatisation (Figley, 2002; Pearlman and Maclan, 1995).

Palliative care social work: making human connections in Covid-19

Sarah Dowd

Sarah Dowd is a practice educator and assessor, as well as a professional and safeguarding lead social worker for a large hospice in the south of England. She has a special interest in resilience among professionals working in palliative care, particularly in terms of participating in important conversations. Below, she reflects upon the impact of the pandemic in a sector where bereavement and loss are already so prevalent.

As I reflect on the last year I struggle to comprehend how much has happened and how quickly we have changed, adapted and adjusted. The best part of my job has been seeing people grow and learn; it's so powerful. In April 2020 I stumbled across the concept of *'vicarious resilience'* as expressed by

Hernandez-Wolfe et al (2007) who reflected what I have found, through witnessing how colleagues and our terminally ill patients and their families found a 'way through'. Alongside the full spectrum of human pain and grief, I have seen change, faith and courage. Their strength has made me feel strong.

Last February I remember trying on PPE and laughing that *'this will never happen... surely we won't need to wear these'*. Now, after a year of wearing PPE, I still loathe it. So much of what you learn at university is about communication, how to listen openly and helpfully. Hidden behind a mask and scrubs, it can still feel a real struggle to create a connection. It can be done and is amazing when it does, but you really have to work hard to make words and other forms of body language convey what usually your face would readily express. I have been really inspired by those colleagues who have communication challenges or a hearing impairment, and how they have somehow found a way to overcome what seemed like impossible barriers.

I have witnessed so much trauma, both first- and second-hand during this year. I watched as a young mum died just as she was being wheeled into our hospice on a stretcher. I comforted the paramedics who were deeply distressed by their experience of taking this young woman from her home on what turned out to be a futile final journey.

As human beings we prepare for death in groups, we grieve in groups and support each other in groups. Now people have had to do this in isolation. In one case I worked with a lady who was dying – her friends could not visit, and her son lived abroad. I never met her when she was conscious, but I will never forget the day I spent with her, and the human connection to her son in another country, where it was the middle of the night. He told me about her favourite music, which I played to her, and I read emails and messages to her from him, while supporting him emotionally over the phone thousands of miles away. Her sister was an actress, and I played a documentary about her. Here, the sun was shining, and I was the live link to her son, so he could let her know how much she meant to him. It felt a real privilege.

Despite this sense of privilege, I have felt angry at the unfairness and injustice for people who couldn't be with the person they loved, though I could. It felt wrong. I understood why on a rational level, but on a human level it felt brutal.

One lady's sisters had travelled from abroad but could not come into the building due to government regulations. We stood in the rain outside as I talked to them about what to expect, and they stood shivering in the doorway as they said goodbye to their sister, who was too drowsy to really engage with them. I have two sisters, and for the first time in my social work career it felt overwhelmingly hard to distance myself from this experience.

Knowing my emotional triggers and being able to acknowledge and navigate transference and boundaries has always been a really important part of my practice (for example, older men crying has always been a big trigger for me!). By knowing what our emotional triggers are, we can create boundaries that help us critically reflect on our actions and reactions. But early in the pandemic I recognised that my emotional triggers had changed. I felt upset by things that would never normally trigger a strong emotional response. I felt afraid: if I couldn't regulate my emotions, I didn't feel 'safe'. Friends and family would often tell me how the work I was doing was amazing and important, and part of me wanted to respond, *'No I am not amazing, I am just hanging by a thread here.'* Some days I felt resentful and desperate to just run away or be on holiday.

I have thought a lot this past year about how I can feel safe in a time of trauma, and support people that need me to be boundaried. In April 2020 I read what Dekel and Baum (2010) had written about *'shared experience'* or *'shared traumatic reality'*. This helped me to understand that I was supporting people in trauma while I was also experiencing trauma and uncertainty. I realised that to create a 'safe space' for them, I needed to feel safe too.

Using supervision as a place to be honest and to be 'Sarah' rather than 'social worker Sarah' has anchored me. Supervision and informal support from colleagues has helped me say the 'unsayable', to speak about experiences and feelings that would otherwise be too terrible to acknowledge. This is what I do; this is social work. But my tolerance has wavered. I came to realise that I was not always patient and understanding when I could have been. I manage and support other social workers, and I would say to them *'Give yourself a break, you are human'*, but wasn't always able to say it to myself. These feelings of guilt and shame can be so powerful and restrictive, making us turn inwards when the very thing needed is openness, which helps us flourish.

In my role I support colleagues from the multi-professional team (eg, nurses, physio and occupational therapists), both formally via clinical supervision and informally. As social workers, colleagues often see us as people who can offer them a safe space. Often my door will open, and a colleague will say, 'Do you have five minutes?' In this pandemic we knew that emotional support was vital for the team, and for several months we ran daily informal reflective sessions. A consistent theme was the secondary trauma or vicarious trauma that people were experiencing, from supporting people who were traumatised by being separated due to Covid-19 and/or were having desperately sad experiences at home or in hospital. Dying is sad for everyone, but against the uncertainty and fear of a pandemic, separation was achingly hard for people. Being among persistent distress and trauma took its toll on all of us (Figley and Abendroth, 2013).

Our team has been a support not only to dying people and their families, but also to each other. Hearing my colleagues in distress and hearing their fear of taking Covid-19 home to their families has been tough. The moral distress they felt between wanting to help others while fearing the virus was intense. It was palpable on the in-patient unit, like electricity humming in the air, every day. Providing that emotional support and reflective space helped me to see what they were overcoming, which gave me hope.

It can be hard to describe what social workers do sometimes, not least in hospices. Social workers see barriers and acknowledge them but say 'Let's give it a go, let's make this happen.' That's what social work is.

I have seen social work practice during this pandemic that is awesome in the truest sense of the word – practice utterly focused on the person and what truly matters to them, whether supporting someone to die at home, or trying to enable communication and connection between families. That's what social workers do; we find *opportunities* where there are barriers. We have hope.

Amid the challenges and stress and paperwork, we *still* have hope. That's why social workers support people to make unwise decisions, that's why social workers agree to educate a student on placement during the middle of a global pandemic, to teach them how to do this job... because we have hope.

You may not always see it (and we don't always feel it) but it's always there, guiding us through.

As Sarah's story highlights, social workers need to be seen as a community of professionals who, in their own right, are likely to be exposed to traumatic events and the physical and emotional aftermath, including PTSD. Creating an organisational culture rooted in a trauma-informed approach, as well as practice 'with' and 'for' social workers, is essential to enable them to carry out their role effectively when responding to disasters and supporting others experiencing trauma.

According to SAMHSA (2014), the four Rs to a trauma-informed approach are as follows.

1. *Realisation* – understanding how trauma can affect children, adults and communities including the workforce.
2. *Recognise* – understand and recognise trauma.
3. *Respond* and apply key principles of trauma-informed approach and practice.
4. *Resist* retraumatisation.

Furthermore, the six key principles of trauma-informed practice (SAMHSA, 2014) are as follows.

1. *Safety* – creating an environment that keeps the workforce and people with lived experience physically and psychologically safe.
2. *Trustworthiness and transparency* – build and maintain trust with the workforce and people with lived experience.
3. *Peer support* – provide choices to the workforce and people with lived experience, and create meaningful engagement in decision-making.
4. *Collaboration and mutuality* – building meaningful relationships.
5. *Empowerment, voice and choice* – share power and give people with lived experience and the workforce a voice in decision-making.
6. *Cultural, historical and gender issues* – responsive to the racial, ethnic, gender, cultural and protected characteristics of individuals served; recognise and address historical trauma.

Covid-19: the profession most hurt by the pandemic

✸ Amadasun (2020) contests that Covid-19 has undermined and at times overturned social work values and that *'if any profession is most hurt by the pandemic, it is the social work profession'*. This is attributed to the importance we place on social justice which is challenged by the disproportionate impact the virus has had on already disadvantaged individuals, groups and communitites.

Recent studies conducted in adult (Manthorpe et al, 2021) and children's services (Baginsky and Manthorpe, 2020) concur in their findings which suggest a general welcome by practitioners to meetings being conducted online but with reservations in respect of limited in-person assessments in terms of reduced quality of information and a negative impact on the development of relationships.

Sen et al (2021) thematically analysed 100 articles which appeared in *SW2020 under Covid-19* online magazine set up during the first UK Covid-19 lockdown period (March–July 2020). Articles were submitted by individuals with lived experience, social workers, students and academics. Four key themes were identified, and Sen et al conclude by outlining an apparent divergence between accounts that suggest improved working relationships between social workers and service users via digital platforms, and other accounts that suggest an increase in a more authoritarian social work approach that has emerged under Covid-19. Despite this divergence, the authors welcome the rise in global activism by the profession and the possibility of community-located social work post-pandemic.

While the introduction and roll out of the vaccination weakens the link between Covid-19 infection and death, the virus will not disappear and continues to infect and rob individuals of their lives. Attention is now being focused upon the lasting effects of the virus, which has become known as the condition 'long Covid'. This is when individuals recover from the initial infection, but the virus continues to have lasting and in some case life-changing impacts on physical and mental health which affect people's ability to resume their 'normal' life and for some their ability to work. The emerging symptoms of the condition include physical symptoms such as fatigue, breathlessness and aching joints as well as mental health impacts such as depression.

A recent study conducted by Imperial College London (Alford, 2021) suggests that one in 20 people have persistent Covid-19 symptoms which will have an impact on social workers and those they work with. Research conducted by the University of Durham and BASW (2021) concludes that social work practice continues to evolve during and after the Covid-19 pandemic and urges social workers to embrace the opportunities that this has presented and manage the impacts of the challenges. We appear to be at a crossroads where, as a profession, social work settles for the 'new normal' which sees a hybrid of office and home working or transforming social work to practice in innovative ways that are underpinned by social justice and compassion (University of Durham and BASW, 2021).

Never a one-off event

A disaster is not a one-off event. There are repercussions for those involved – families, friends and communities live with the ripples of the disaster on a daily basis. Anniversaries of disasters, which are often commemorated either privately or publicly in the news, serve to remember the loss of loved ones. However, as newspapers republish photographs and we scroll through social media posts, we should be mindful that, despite the good intentions, these images can also act as a retraumatising reminder to survivors and their families. The stories so generously shared by the contributors in this book reflect not only the deep distress felt by people in experiencing the loss of loved ones and those in their communities but how the subsequent experience of loss can be silenced through injustice and lack of action. For those who have lost members of their families, friends or community, the pain and memories remain with them. Subsequent public inquiries and legal processes, while essential in terms of gaining a sense of justice and revealing the truth, serve as a constant reminder of the pain and loss over a prolonged period of time as these processes are lengthy to conduct and resolve. During the writing of this book, we were reminded of the prolonged nature of disasters as inquests and legal hearings into the Hillsborough football disaster and Manchester Arena bombing continue.

During the latter stages of writing this book, we are aware of two people who survived disasters but then went on to lose their lives as a result of their experience. On 29 July 2021, it was reported that Andrew Devine, aged 55, who died 32 years after enduring severe and irreversible brain damage at Hillsborough in 1989, was unlawfully killed, and so became the 97th victim of the disaster (Conn and Vinter, 2021). Similarly, on 9 August 2021, it was announced that Eve Aston, aged 20, a survivor of the Manchester Arena bombing, was found dead in her bedroom. Although the cause of her death remains unknown, the family have talked of Eve's struggles with loud noises and sleeping since the concert (Hall, 2021). Again, a sad reminder that disasters can irreversibly change people's lives and those around them.

Striving to achieve accountability through the English justice system is often a lonely, long and inequitable process. This has been particularly highlighted by the Hillsborough families who, while grieving the loss of loved ones, found themselves in court, with barely any legal representation, up against highly paid QCs, employed by public bodies 'not always seeking to establish the truth but to protect reputations' (Burnham, 2021). Andy Burnham, mayor of Greater Manchester, who has long campaigned for justice for and with the Hillsborough families, presented the Public Authority (Accountability) Bill to Parliament. The Bill has two core recommendations: parity of legal funding for bereaved families, and a duty of candour on public officials. It proposes to make it illegal for those in public service to give misleading information and penalties and fines for those wilfully non-compliant. Second, the Bill advocates for a level playing field, promoting those families, victims and survivors to be permitted resources for representation at public inquests. Margaret Aspinall told her story of the loss of her son James at Hillsborough in Chapter 3, and has spoken elsewhere about having to use the money she received from the Criminal Injuries Compensation scheme in respect of James to pay her contribution to the families' legal fund. This was insufficient and so Margaret turned to her parents to borrow more money to pay for one barrister at the first Hillsborough inquest (Burnham, 2021). The Bill was expected to have a second reading debate on 12 May 2017 but as a general election was called and Parliament was dissolved from 3 May 2017, the Bill falls and no further action was taken (Parliamentary Bills, 2017).

Legacy of disasters in England

As a profession, social work is reflective in nature and frequently reconsiders significant or tragic events and strives to learn lessons from them – examples of this include Serious Case Reviews established under the Children Act

(2004). Disaster work is no different in this regard, where survivors and their friends and families campaign for changes in policy, procedure and law to prevent a similar tragedy reoccurring. Equally the bereaved and survivors strive for justice and accountability through public inquiries and court proceedings. Under pressure from campaigning groups, governments are often forced to consider changes to legislation, policy, and procedure. This is particularly relevant to the Kegworth air crash, Hillsborough football disaster, Grenfell Tower fire and the Manchester Arena bombing.

Kegworth air crash

The Kegworth aeroplane crash resulted in several aviation safety recommendations that include improved co-ordination between cabin crew and flight deck, and the introduction of passenger safety briefings with particular significance being placed on the importance of adopting the correct 'brace' position (Calder, 2020).

Hillsborough disaster

The many ways in which the justice system continues to fail the families, survivors and victims of Hillsborough is well documented. However, the Hillsborough disaster significantly changed the experience of attending football matches in England. Any individual attending a Premier League football match must now have an allocated seat and every stadium, by law, must have a seat for everyone in attendance. Hillsborough outstrips football and is more than goals, dribbles and tackles – yet football is a sport that can unite rather than divide as those seeking justice have reminded us for decades. Court cases resulting from the aftermath of the Hillsborough tragedy have helped shape healthcare law in the UK. Law relating to claims for psychiatric injury have changed as courts now accept that claims for psychiatric injury are regarded the same as claims for other forms of injury under the law of negligence (Griffin, 2014).

In the decades following the Hillsborough disaster, a Charter for Families Bereaved through Public Tragedy was created. The Charter is made up of a series of commitments by public bodies to change their conduct in relation to transparency and acting in the public interest (Gov.uk, 2017).

Grenfell Tower fire

Following the Grenfell Tower fire, more than 400 high-rise buildings in England were identified as having unsafe composite material (ACM) external cladding similar to that which failed with tragic consequences at Grenfell. The government made £200 million available for the replacement of the unsafe ACM cladding on high-rise residential dwellings in the social and private sector and interim measures to ensure safety measures were implemented by local authorities and the fire and rescue services. Following the 2017 Grenfell Tower blaze in which 72 people lost their lives, the Fire Safety Act (2021) was introduced, aimed at making homes safer. However, a push to include more financial protection for leaseholders was defeated in Parliament, leaving leaseholders facing hefty bills to pay for protective measures such as fire breaks, non-combustible balconies, safer doors and sprinkler systems. The government has announced the Building Safety Fund, which is a welcome step towards the acknowledgement of a need for resources to fund the remediation of buildings clad in products other than the ACM used on Grenfell Tower. However, the Fund has significant limitations as it is restricted to buildings over 17.7m in height. This leaves approximately 88,000 buildings with no recourse to funding. People living in properties across England with cladding describe feeling trapped in homes they once cherished but they can no longer sell because lenders will not offer mortgages until the cladding is removed (BBC, 2021b). This is not just about resources but more about the value, as a society, we place upon life, as those without money are unlikely to be in a position to make their home safe.

Manchester Arena bombing

Martyn Hett lost his life in the terror attack at Manchester Arena in 2017. Since his death, his mother Figen Murray has been lobbying the government to bring in new security measures, advocating for 'Martyn's Law' as existing legislative measures are deemed inadequate. The new proposals, which are currently being considered by the Home Office, would create a comprehensive and proportionate approach to protective security for venues. The proposed requirements include that those employed by venues engage in counterterrorism training and advice, conduct vulnerability assessments, mitigate any potential risk and produce a counterterrorism plan. There is also a proposed requirement for local authorities to plan for the threat of terrorism (BBC, 2020). Since the 2017 attack, backpacks and large bags have been banned from large concert venues, but there is no legal requirement for public venues to conduct security checks.

Media and disasters

The media has historically been used to communicate disaster events be it through the medium of radio or newspapers; however, in a global age the nature of disasters is transforming. Highly transmissible pandemics, climate change and terrorist attacks mean that disasters are no longer contained geographically. The powerful machine that is the media plays a critical role in contributing to not only the coverage of disasters but ongoing discussions over how society responds. Within a global context, the media *shapes disasters from the* inside out, *and* outside in' in terms of the ebb and flow of communication (Cottle, 2014).

It can be argued that communication through the media now transcends space and time in an unparalleled manner. Cottle (2014) argues that the extensity and intensity of media and communications globally are characterised by six distinct features: scale, speed, saturation, social relations, surveillance and seeing. Scale and speed relate to the global impact that new digital technologies and the internet have on us by exposing us to images and words worldwide on many platforms, including social media, instantaneously as disasters unfold. The advent of the mobile phone has provided us with the ability to become saturated by disaster events as they are happening regardless of where we are or what we might be doing. New technologies have given us access to disasters from the perspective of those involved – be they survivors, professionals, witnesses or relief workers, and so provide a social aspect to the events. This in turn supports the media to take on a surveillance role and reduce the potential attempts of those in authorities to conceal the truth or downplay the severity of the situation. Lastly the cameras on mobile phones have increased the imagery and visual representation of disasters as we 'bear witness' in real time to the horror as it unfolds before our eyes (Cottle, 2014).

Typically, disaster reporting, especially at the time and in the immediate aftermath, seeks to establish facts such as the number of fatalities and casualties, the apparent cause and who to apportion blame to. The images of the horrors of the Hillsborough disaster entered people's homes as the football match was being televised live. We can only imagine the distress and fear felt by those watching this match knowing a loved one was there in the crowd. The media and in particular the newspapers were extremely hostile to Liverpool football supporters and held them responsible for the disaster. Initial coverage focused on football hooliganism, which was a significant political issue at the time, and alcohol consumption, which distorted the truth and added to the burden of grieving families, friends and the city of Liverpool. Writing in 2010, Jemphrey and Berrington (p 479) conclude that:

> in disaster reporting, journalists are under pressure to produce copy quickly and to dramatize and sensationalize what are already dramatic stories. In complying with these editorial demands, the rights and expectations of bereaved people and survivors are endangered, and sensitivity is sacrificed to the business and managerial imperatives of publishing.

This approach has had far-reaching consequences and has taken survivors of the Hillsborough disaster many years of campaigning for justice for the truth to be formally revealed and acknowledged. Finally, a verdict of unlawful killing has been announced where a series of failures by the police and ambulance service contributed to the disaster. This confirmed that the Liverpool fans were wholly blameless for the tragedy that occurred in Hillsborough.

In his report of the Manchester Arena bombing, Lord Kerslake heard that families felt 'hounded' and 'bombarded' by the media. Survivors of the bombing have accused journalists of unethical practice including bribing hospital staff for stories, gaining access to victims by impersonating professionals and taking intrusive photographs (BBC, 2018). Journalists have a moral and professional responsibility to strike a balance between the public interest in reporting disaster events and considering the impact of any intrusion their coverage may have on the individual, families and communities. Following this report, the Independent Press Standards Organisation has published new guidance for journalists and editors on reporting of major incidents, which highlights issues surrounding accuracy, privacy, harassment, intrusion into grief or shock, children and hospitals (IPSO, 2019).

The public and political appetite for journalism regulations is not new – rather, the establishment of IPSO guidelines marks one step forward in a long history of tension between the media and its subjects. The former has tended to privilege both freedom of expression and public interest over right to privacy, to which the latter has continuously objected. The National Union of Journalists suggested a regulatory system following the Second World War, which went unheeded, and it was only after the threat of statutory control from the government that the Press Council – a voluntary organisation dedicated to maintaining high standards of journalism ethics – was established (Foley, 1997). While the British media has managed to remain free of governmental control, it still fails to live up to its position as an objective, neutral force in reporting, and is influenced by other major players. According to a report on media ownership in the United Kingdom, just three companies – DMG Media, News UK and Reach – dominate 90 per cent of the national newspaper market, up from 83 per cent in 2019 (Media Reform Coalition, 2021).

As such, a small minority of wealthy and highly influential stakeholders are afforded the power to set the agenda for the press (and ultimately public discourse). According to research by the National Council for the Training of Journalists (NCTJ), 90 per cent of those working in UK newsrooms are white and 75 per cent are from the highest social class (NCTJ, 2021), which further divorces the press from the reality of what disaster survivors, who are disproportionately from disadvantaged backgrounds, experience. Survivors are therefore left with no guarantee that those who think or look like them exist within newsrooms, leaving them at risk of lacking advocates within institutions that seek to sensationalise their stories. The voices of the marginalised remain unheard and misrepresented – and the prognosis for the social workers who support them is not much brighter.

The relationship between social workers and the media is compounded by the pre-existing tension between the press and the social work profession. The media privileges news stories which carry profit potential, and this sadly rules out much of the positive work social workers undertake both within and outside of disaster contexts. It has been suggested that instead, the media opts for 'social work's bad news [which] provides sex and violence in abundance' (Aldridge, 1990, p 612). This in turn spins the pervasive narrative that social work functions as 'a sinister arm of the state, focused on the systematic removal of children above all else' (Mason, 2018). Social workers are portrayed in a binary sense as either meddling unnecessarily in family life, or failing to intervene when needed.

The press pendulum may swing from criticising social workers for their over- or under-involvement, but its 'hostile' attitude remains unchanged. In 2006, a literature review on media representations of social work found that such hostility has been a constant position since the 1970s (Galilee, 2006). The deaths of Victoria Climbié in 2000 and Baby P in 2007 (among other lesser reported child deaths) intensified such hostility. In his 2009 progress report on the protection of children in England, commissioned to evaluate the good practice developed since the Independent Statutory Inquiry following the death of Victoria Climbié, Lord Laming noted a *long term appetite in the media to portray social workers in ways that are negative and undermining* (Laming, 2009).

The increase in hostility toward social workers, combined with the advent of new technologies in the mid- to late 2000s, created a perfect storm in which public discontent toward the profession could thrive. For the first time in history, readers could comment on, share or 'like' content in real-time. Rather than passively consuming content, they were invited into a bi-directional transaction with the press. News organisations galvanised the new active role readers could take, using comment sections to dramatic effect to engage audiences in articles relating to Baby P (Jones, 2012). This interactive engagement culminated in an e-petition by the *Sun* newspaper, which called for the dismissal of Haringey's head of Children's Services, among others, which was based on erroneous information. With 1.4 million signatures, it was the biggest in newspaper history at that time (Greenslade, 2012). No equivalent petition was made regarding the other multi-agency professionals involved with Baby P, demonstrating the extent to which social workers were uniquely targeted in the press.

It is unsurprising, then, that years of disparaging media commentary about social workers has eroded public confidence in the profession. Perhaps what the media fails to realise is that when social workers are scapegoated, those they support suffer by proxy. In Laming's progress report on the protection of children in England, written to measure the impact of recommendations made in the Independent Statutory Inquiry following the death of Victoria Climbié, he stated that public vilification of social workers *has a negative impact on staff and has serious implications for the effectiveness, status and morale of the children's workforce as a whole* (Laming, 2009, p 44). In the same year, a survey by *Community Care* found that 40 per cent of those who took part said the Baby P case was impacting on their professional practice (Ahmed, 2008).

In the absence of positive news stories about social work, the narrative surrounding the profession has not evolved, and the public will continue to have a disproportionately negative understanding of the role. Even when presented with opportunities to spotlight the good work undertaken by social workers (the coronavirus being a prime example, when practitioners made enormous sacrifices to serve communities), the media tends to turn a blind eye. The difference in media coverage of the efforts made by social workers compared to allied professionals was striking. The latter were hailed as key worker heroes – and rightly so – but equivalent praise for social workers was absent. Whether or not this is a coincidence remains uncertain; however, the media leaves much to be desired when it comes to fairly portraying the profession. Social workers do not enter the profession for praise, but recognition is essential to a sense of staff well-being, morale and purpose.

There are positive examples of how powerful instant communication can be when using smartphones and social media. As well as providing instantaneous news stories, social media, in a time of disaster, has proved to be a place where services of help are offered including shelter and support. In the immediate aftermath of the Manchester Arena bombing, individuals using the Facebook social media platform could check into a special service to record that they were safe, or where people might become separated at events and so offer a sense of reassurance amid chaos and confusion. There is also a darker side of social media, where deliberate false stories and misinformation is posted, reposted and shared, spreading the 'fake news' to millions around the world.

What next for social work in disasters?

It is incumbent upon us to amplify the voices of colleagues, individuals, families and communities that have experienced a disaster and continue to try to make sense of their lives following the tragic event. The memory of the disaster for survivors will remain and so we must take from them the messages that have been eloquently and generously shared by the contributors in this book. In summary these messages include the following.

- Those who have survived a disaster might not always understand the role of the social worker. It is up to us as a profession to collectively explain our role and remit.

- We must use our social work skills to actively listen, to help people find alternative solutions.

- Do not underestimate the power of collective and community strength and resilience to achieve justice.

- Support communities to rebuild their lives.

- Offer services that are not restricted within tight timeframes as people experience disasters in different ways and survive in many ways.

- Working in a disaster is emotionally and physically demanding. Ensure that you are able to provide the support that others might need.

- Practise self-care.

- Engage in training and learning around disaster work.

Reflective questions

- How has your understanding of trauma, in its many forms, been affected by reading this chapter?

- What can you do to influence change in this area of work? How might you connect with others to make a difference?

Barusch (2011, p 348) states that disaster preparedness is an *'oxymoron... if we were prepared it wouldn't have been a disaster, would it?'* In some respects, this assertion is true, that some disasters are totally unexpected and demand an immediate response which might, in retrospect, not be the most helpful or effective. Yet, there are times when, as a society, we ignore warning signs or expert opinions such as the clear indicators of the potential disaster looming if we do not collectively address global climate change and live more sustainably. Similarly, it would be disrespectful to every person who has lost their lives and every survivor who campaigns for justice if we do not learn from the past to make us more prepared and responsive.

One of the key messages from contributors of this book is the need to not only provide clarity around the role of the social worker in disaster work, but also for practitioners to engage in learning and training around disasters. BASW promotes training in disaster work for social workers as part of their continuous professional development so that practitioners are more able to fulfil their role in disaster preparedness, response and recovery. This will enable them to apply legislation and policy to this context while practising in a research informed manner underpinned by relevant theories and models. By doing this, social workers are more likely to truly come out of the shadows and be able to fully understand the devastating impact of disasters on individuals, families and communities, and so be able to reflect on the wider contexts, cause and implications while prioritising the perspectives of people who have been impacted by a disaster.

Taking it further

If you want to become more engaged in social work in disasters, there are a number of campaigning organisations that you can join or become involved with.

Grenfell United	www.grenfellunited.org.uk
Justice4Grenfell	www.justice4grenfell.org
Grenfell Foundation	www.grenfellfoundation.org.uk
Hillsborough Justice Campaign	www.contrast.org/hillsborough
Hillsborough Survivors Support Alliance	www.hsa-us.co.uk
Covid Families for Justice	www.covidfamiliesforjustice.org
Manchester Arena Survivors	www.peace-foundation.org.uk

Look at me

Poem by Tashinga Matewe written for the BASW England Annual Members Meeting, 9 June 2021

Look at me and tell me what do you see,

Maybe, a young black girl, speaking confident and clean?

Or maybe just a girl filled with aspirations and dreams?

But in reality we all know that things aren't quite as they seem.

See I'm also another young person who's been affected by covid 19,

Confused about the future, past and all that comes in-between

Also another young person affected by my race that makes me, me

Living in a society that still puts negative emphasis on the race of my skin.

It's crazy because this world got me feeling like I can't win.

We're being made breathless by the pandemic while our brother's necks were crushed, being made breathless by a police officer's knee.

We were forced to pick between our safety from this infectious disease

and protesting against the plague of racial inequalities.

We were told to reside inside our homes so we could stay safe,

Yet we weren't told how to preserve our mental states

We were facing internal battles that we have never faced,

None of which could simply be helped by track and trace.

→

It's been hard, so so hard

Trying to adapt to this new abstract version of normality.

We're living in a brand new reality,

Where we have to wear masks and socially distance

While we speak facts and protest against the social resistance

on our human rights.

The ones that are supposed to be there to protect our human lives

And it's hard to figure out what it is that is right.

Should I protest against the things that I know ain't right,

The type of things that have plagued our human lives?

Or stay home in hopes that I'm part of the fight,

To stop covid from taking any more innocent lives.

There's so many different aspects to this long unruly trial

It's physically and emotionally draining and it's been like this for a while

But we need to stay positive and know that everything will end up alright

Its tough tryna get through this life but I know we won't go down without a fight

Even though it's like we've been trapped in a never ending game,

With thousands of levels that have been filled with everlasting pain,

We can get through this.

You see we're stronger than this, all of this

we need to get rid of the fogs of uncertainty and anxiety
that have been all around us

and find a way to make real change about us.

It's all about trust

Trusting each other and trusting ourselves

We're one step closer to getting that long-awaited
better health

That glorious mental wealth

And that spiritual healing that really could help.

So let's not put our heads down and decide that we're done

even though we're feeling like we're staring down
the barrel of a gun

because we're more than that

We need to fight until we've won

And show the world what's right and let it be done,

This strange part of our lives has made true history,

but it's time we break ourselves out of this misery.

We can be united through the pain,

and make sure it doesn't leave a tainted stain.

Together we stand, divided we fall

I just want to know if you're down for it all.

References

ADASS and BASW (2019) Response and Recommendations from the Task and Finish Groups Looking at: The Role of the DASS and Social Workers in Disaster Recovery. [online] Available at: www.basw.co.uk/system/files/resources/ADASS%20-%20BASW%20Joint%20Statement%20on%20the%20role%20of%20SW%20as%20Keyworker.pdf (accessed 11 January 2022).

Age International (2018) Older People in Emergencies. [online] Available at: www.ageinternational.org.uk/policy-research/expert-voices/older-people-in-emergencies/ (accessed 11 January 2022).

Ahmed, M (2008) Baby P Survey: Social Workers Say Case Affects their Own Job. *Community Care*, 11 November. [online] Available at: www.communitycare.co.uk/2008/11/18/baby-p-survey-social-workers-say-case-affects-their-own-jobs/ (accessed 11 January 2022).

Al-Dahash, H, Thayaparan, M and Kulatunga, U (2016) Understanding the Terminologies: Disaster, Crisis and Emergency. In *The 32nd Annual ARCOM Conference* (pp 1191–200). Manchester: Association of Researchers in Construction Management.

Aldridge, M (1990) Social Work and the News Media: A Hopeless Case? *British Journal of Social Work*, 20(6): 611–25.

Alford, J (2021) Over 2 Million Adults in England May Have Had Long Covid – Imperial REACT. [online] Available at: www.imperial.ac.uk/news/224853/over-million-adults-england-have-long/ (accessed 11 January 2022).

Allen, R (2020) Four Ways the Covid-19 Crisis Will Transform UK Social Work. *The Guardian*, 24 June. [online] Available at: www.theguardian.com/society/2020/jun/24/covid-19-crisis-transform-social-work (accessed 11 January 2022).

Alston, M, Hazeleger, T and Hargreaves, D (2019) *Social Work and Disasters: A Handbook for Practice.* London: Routledge.

Amadasun, S (2020) Social Work and COVID-19 Pandemic: An Action Call. *International Social Work*, 63(6): 753–6.

Amnesty International (2020) Policing the Pandemic: Human Rights Violations in the Enforcement of Covid-19 Measures in Europe. [online] Available at: www.amnesty.org/en/documents/eur01/2511/2020/en/ (accessed 11 January 2022).

Baginsky, M and Manthorpe, J (2020) The Impact of Covid-19 on Children's Social Care in England. *Child Abuse and Neglect*. [online] Available at: www.ncbi.nlm.nih.gov/pmc/articles/PMC7494292/ (accessed 11 January 2022).

Barusch, A S (2011) Disaster, Vulnerability, and Older Adults: Toward a Social Work Response. *Journal of Gerontological Social Work*, 54(4): 347–50.

BASW (2018) Professional Capabilities Framework. [online] Available at: www.basw.co.uk/social-work-training/professional-capabilities-framework-pcf (accessed 11 January 2022).

BASW (2020a) Quick Guide: Self-Care for Social Workers during Covid-19. 27 April. [online] Available at: www.basw.co.uk/quick-guide-self-care-social-workers-during-covid-19#:~:text=%20Guidance%20for%20Individuals%20%201%20Check%20in,system%2C%20consider%20writing%20notes%20in%20word...%20More%20 (accessed 11 January 2022).

BASW (2020b) Upholding Human Rights during Covid-19. 24 June [online] Available at: www.basw.co.uk/media/news/2020/jun/upholding-human-rights-during-covid-19 (accessed 11 January 2022).

BASW (2021a) Social Work during the Covid-19 Pandemic: Initial Findings. 28 January. [online] Available at: www.basw.co.uk/resources/social-work-during-covid-19-pandemic-initial-findings (accessed 11 January 2022).

BASW (2021b) Code of Ethics. [online] Available at: www.basw.co.uk/about-basw/code-ethics (accessed 11 January 2022).

BASW (nd) Manchester Survivors Choir. [online] Available at: www.basw.co.uk/social-work-disasters/manchester-survivors-choir (accessed 11 January 2022).

Baum, N (2014) Professionals' Double Exposure in the Shared Traumatic Reality of Wartime: Contributions to Professional Growth and Stress. *British Journal of Social Work*, 44(8): 2113–34.

Bauwens, J and Naturale, A (2017) The Role of Social Work in the Aftermath of Disasters and Traumatic Events. *Clinical Social Work Journal*, 45(2): 99–101.

BBC (2018) Manchester Arena Bombing: Key Points from the Official Report. 27 March. [online] Available at: www.bbc.co.uk/news/uk-england-43554555 (accessed 11 January 2022).

BBC (2020) Help Us Make Venues Safer, Urges Bomb Victim's Mum. 24 February. [online] Available at: www.bbc.co.uk/news/uk-51607042 (accessed 11 January 2022).

BBC (2021a) Everyone's Invited: Met Investigates School Abuse Claims Made on Website. 26 March. [online] Available at: www.bbc.co.uk/news/uk-england-london-56545081 (accessed 11 January 2022).

BBC (2021b) Grenfell: Survivors Condemn New Fire Safety Laws. 29 April. [online] Available at: www.bbc.co.uk/news/uk-politics-56924131 (accessed 11 January 2022).

Beinecke, R, Raymond, A, Cisse, M, Renna, K, Khan, S, Fuller, A and Crawford, K (2017) The Mental Health Response to the Boston Bombing: A Three-Year Review. *International Journal of Mental Health*, 46(2): 89–124.

BMA (2020) Vicarious Trauma: Signs and Strategies for Coping. [online] Available at: www.bma.org.uk/advice-and-support/your-wellbeing/vicarious-trauma/vicarious-trauma-signs-and-strategies-for-coping (accessed 11 January 2022).

Bradshaw, S and Fordham, M (2013) Women, Girls and Disasters: A Review for DFID. [online] Available at: https://assets.publishing.service.gov.uk/government/uploads/system/uploads/attachment_data/file/844489/withdrawn-women-girls-disasters.pdf (accessed 11 January 2022).

Bride, B E (2007) Prevalence of Secondary Traumatic Stress among Social Workers. *Social Work*, 52(1): 63–70.

Burnham, A (2020) Andy Burnham Writes to Robert Jenrick over 'Everyone In' Homelessness Policy. [online] Available at: www.greatermanchester-ca.gov.uk/news/andy-burnham-writes-to-robert-jenrick-over-everyone-in-homelessness-policy/ (accessed 11 January 2022).

Burnham, A (2021) The Collapse of the Last Hillsborough Trial Shows Our Legal System is Broken. *The Guardian*, 30 May. [online] Available at: www.theguardian.com/commentisfree/2021/may/30/collapse-hillsborough-trial-legal-system-law-bereaved-family-trauma-court (accessed 11 January 2022).

Calder, S (2020) Kegworth: The Lessons Learnt from the Last UK Air Disaster. *Independent*, 29 January. [online] Available at: www.independent.co.uk/travel/news-and-advice/kegworth-30-years-uk-air-disaster-crash-british-midland-boeing-737-fatal-accident-a8717161.html (accessed 11 January 2022).

Care Quality Commission (2020) Review of Do Not Attempt Cardiopulmonary Resuscitation Decisions during the Covid-19 Pandemic. [online] Available at: www.cqc.org.uk/sites/default/files/20201204%20DNACPR%20Interim%20Report%20-%20FINAL.pdf (accessed 11 January 2022).

Cleary, J and Dominelli, L (2020) *Social Work and Disasters: Systematic Literature Review*. Stirling, Scotland: University of Stirling, Faculty of Social Sciences.

Conn, D and Vinter, R (2021) Liverpool Fan's Death Ruled as 97th of Hillsborough Disaster. *The Guardian*, 29 July. [online] Available at: www.theguardian.com/football/2021/jul/28/liverpool-fans-death-ruled-as-97th-victim-of-hillsborough-disaster (accessed 11 January 2022).

Cooper, L, Briggs, L and Bagshaw, S (2018) Postdisaster Counselling: Personal, Professional, and Ethical Issues. *Australian Social Work*, 71(4): 430–43.

Cottle, S (2014) Rethinking Media and Disasters in a Global Age: What's Changed and Why it Matters. *Media, War and Conflict*, 7(1): 3–22.

Dekel, R and Baum, N (2010) Intervention in a Shared Traumatic Reality: A New Challenge for Social Workers. *British Journal of Social Work*, 40(6): 1927–44.

Department for Education (2021) Guidance: Children of Critical Workers and Vulnerable Children Who Can Access Schools or Educational Settings. [online] Available at: www.gov.uk/government/publications/coronavirus-covid-19-maintaining-educational-provision/guidance-for-schools-colleges-and-local-authorities-on-maintaining-educational-provision (accessed 11 January 2022).

Department of Health and Social Care (2020) Coronavirus (Covid-19) Action Plan. [online] Available at: www.gov.uk/government/publications/coronavirus-action-plan (accessed 11 January 2022).

Department of Health and Social Care and Public Health England (2020) Coronavirus (COVID-19): Adult Social Care Guidance. [online] Available at: www.gov.uk/government/collections/coronavirus-covid-19-social-care-guidance (accessed 11 January 2022).

Dominelli, L (2011) Climate Change: Social Workers' Contributions to Policy and Practice Debates. *International Journal of Social Welfare*, 20(4): 430–9.

Dominelli, L (2012) *Green Social Work: From Environmental Degradation to Environmental Justice*. Cambridge: Polity Press.

Dominelli, L (2014) Disaster Interventions and Humanitarian Aid Guidelines, Toolkits and Manual. Durham University. [online] Available at: www.erra.gov.pk/media/Articale%202016/Disaster%20Interventions%20Tool%20Kit.pdf (accessed 11 January 2022).

Dominelli, L (2015) The Opportunities and Challenges of Social Work Interventions in Disaster Situations. *International Social Work*, 58(5): 659–72.

Dominelli, L (2018) Green Social Work and the Uptake by the Nepal School of Social Work: Building Resilience in Disaster-Stricken Communities. In Bracken, L and Ruszczyk, H (eds) *Evolving Narratives of Hazard and Risk: The Gorkha Earthquake, Nepal 2015* (pp 141–58). London: Palgrave Macmillan.

Dominelli, L and Ioakimidis, V (2015) Social Work on the Frontline in Addressing Disasters, Social Problems and Marginalization. *International Social Work*, 58(1): 3–6.

Ellor, J and Mayo, M C (2018) Congregational and Social Work Responses to Older Survivors of Natural/Human Disasters. *Social Work and Christianity*, 45(1): 42–59.

Eyre, A and Dix, P (2014) *Collective Conviction: The Story of Disaster Action.* Liverpool: Liverpool University Press.

Figley, C R (2002) Introduction. In Figley, C R (ed) *Treating Compassion Fatigue.* New York: Brunner-Routledge.

Figley, C R and Abendroth, M (2013) *Trauma and the Therapeutic Relationship: Approaches to Process and Practice.* Basingstoke: Palgrave Macmillan.

Foley, M (1997) The Princess and Privacy. *Index on Censorship*, 26(5): 162–3.

Galilee, J (2006) Literature Review on Media Representation of Social Work. [online] Available at: www.socialworkscotland.org.uk/resources/pub/SocialWorkersandtheMedia.pdf (accessed 11 January 2022).

Gentleman, A (2017) Grenfell Tower MP Highlights Huge Social Divisions in London. *The Guardian.* [online] Available at: www.theguardian.com/inequality/2017/nov/13/grenfell-tower-mp-highlights-huge-social-divisions-in-london (accessed 14 February 2022).

Gibson, M (2006) *Order from Chaos: Responding to Traumatic Events.* Bristol: Policy Press.

Gov.uk (2017) Bishop's Review of Hillsborough Families' Experiences Published. [online] Available at: www.gov.uk/government/news/bishops-review-of-hillsborough-families-experiences-published (accessed 11 January 2022).

Greenslade, R (2012) The *Sun* Changes its Stance, Yet Again, Over the Baby P Case. *The Guardian*, 2 August. [online] Available at: www.theguardian.com/media/greenslade/2012/aug/02/sun-baby-p (accessed 11 January 2022).

Griffin, R (2014) The Hillsborough Disaster: How it Changed UK Health Care Law, Part 1. *British Journal of Nursing*, 23(10): 536–7.

Hall, L (2020) Everyone In. [online] Available at: https://assets.publishing.service.gov.uk/government/uploads/system/uploads/attachment_data/file/876466/Letter_from_Minister_Hall_to_Local_Authorities.pdf (accessed 11 January 2022).

Hall, R (2021) Woman Who Survived Manchester Arena Bombing Found Dead in Bedroom. *The Guardian*, 9 August. [online] Available at: www.theguardian.com/uk-news/2021/aug/09/woman-who-survived-manchester-arena-bombing-found-dead-in-bedroom (accessed 11 January 2022).

Hernandez-Wolfe, P, Gangsei, D and Engstrom, D (2007) Vicarious Resilience: A New Concept in Work with those who Survive Trauma. *Family Process*, 46: 229–41.

Hopper, E K, Bassuk, E L and Olivet, J (2010) Shelter from the Storm: Trauma-Informed Care in Homelessness Services. *The Open Health Services and Policy Journal*, 3: 80–100.

House of Commons (2021a) The Adoption and Children (Coronavirus) (Amendment) Regulations. Briefing Paper Number 8934. 10 March. [online] Available at: https://researchbriefings.files.parliament.uk/documents/CBP-8934/CBP-8934.pdf (accessed 11 January 2022).

House of Commons (2021b) Coronavirus: Lessons Learned to Date. Sixth Report of the Health and Social Care Committee and Third Report of the Science and Technology Committee of Session 2021–22. 12 October. [online] Available at: https://committees.parliament.uk/publications/7496/documents/78687/default/ (accessed 11 January 2022).

IFRC (2020) What Is a Disaster? [online] Available at: www.ifrc.org/en/what-we-do/disaster-management/about-disasters/what-is-a-disaster/#:~:text=A%20disaster%20is%20a%20sudden,cope%20using%20its%20own%20resources (accessed 11 January 2022).

IFSW (2014) Global Definition of Social Work. [online] Available at: www.ifsw.org/what-is-social-work/global-definition-of-social-work/ (accessed 11 January 2022).

IPSO (2019) Reporting Major Incidents. [online] Available at: www.ipso.
co.uk/member-publishers/guidance-for-journalists-and-editors/reporting-
major-incidents/ (accessed 11 January 2022).

Jemphrey, A and Berrington, E (2010) Surviving the Media: Hillsborough,
Dunblane and the Press. *Journalism Studies*, 1(3): 469–83.

Jones, R (2012) Child Protection, Social Work and the Media: Doing as Well
as Being Done To. *Research, Policy and Planning*, 29(2): 83–94.

Joubert, L, Hocking, A and Hampson, R (2013) Social Work in Oncology:
Managing Vicarious Trauma – The Positive Impact of Professional
Supervision. *Social Work in Health Care*, 52(2–3): 296–310.

Klein, N (2008) *The Shock Doctrine*. Toronto: Random House.

Laming, H (2009) *The Protection of Children: A Progress Report*. London:
The Stationery Office.

Legislation.gov.uk (2020a) Coronavirus Act 2020. [online] Available at: www.
legislation.gov.uk/ukpga/2020/7/contents/enacted (accessed 11 January 2022).

Legislation.gov.uk (2020b) The Adoption and Children (Coronavirus)
(Amendment) Regulations 2020. [online] Available at: www.legislation.gov.
uk/uksi/2020/445/contents/made (accessed 11 January 2022).

Manthorpe, J, Harris, J, Burridge, S, Fuller, J, Martineau, S, Ornelas, B, Tinelli,
M and Cornes, M (2021) Social Work Practice with Adults under the Rising
Second Wave of Covid-19 in England: Frontline Experiences and the Use of
Professional Judgement. *The British Journal of Social Work*, 51(5): 1879–96.

Mason, S (2018) A Warped View of Social Work in the Media is
Unfair – and Dangerous. *The Guardian*, 16 May. [online] Available
at: www.theguardian.com/social-care-network/social-life-blog/2018/may/
16/media-social-work-press-state-children (accessed 11 January 2022).

Mauro, C, Reynolds, C, Maercker, A, Skritskaya, N, Simon, N, Zisook, S
and Shear, M (2019) Prolonged Grief Disorder: Clinical Utility of ICD-11
Diagnostic Guidelines. *Psychological Medicine*, 49(5): 861–7.

Media Reform Coalition (2021) Who Owns the UK Media? [online] Available
at: www.mediareform.org.uk/wp-content/uploads/2021/03/Who-Owns-
the-UK-Media_final2.pdf (accessed 11 January 2022).

Mencap (2021) Eight in 10 Deaths of People with a Learning Disability are Covid Related as Inequality Soars. [online] Available at: www.mencap.org.uk/press-release/eight-10-deaths-people-learning-disability-are-covid-related-inequality-soars (accessed 11 January 2022).

Michalopoulos, L M and Aparicio, E (2012) Vicarious Trauma in Social Workers: The Role of Trauma History, Social Support, and Years of Experience. *Journal of Aggression, Maltreatment and Trauma*, 21(6): 646–64.

Moore-Bick, M (2019) Grenfell Tower Inquiry: Phase 1 Report Overview Fire at Grenfell Tower on 14 June 2017. [online] Available at: https://assets.grenfelltowerinquiry.org.uk/GTI%20-%20Phase%201%20report%20Executive%20Summary.pdf (accessed 11 January 2022).

Myers, D and Wee, D (2005) *Disaster Mental Health Services*. New York: Brunner-Routledge.

Naturale, A (2007) Secondary Traumatic Stress in Social Workers Responding to Disasters: Reports from the Field. *Clinical Social Work*, 35: 173–81.

NCTJ (2021) Diversity in Journalism: An Update on the Characteristics of Journalists. [online] Available at: www.nctj.com/downloadlibrary/Diversity%20in%20journalism%202021.pdf (accessed 11 January 2022).

NHS (2018) Symptoms – Post-Traumatic Stress Disorder. [online] Available at: www.nhs.uk/mental-health/conditions/post-traumatic-stress-disorder-ptsd/symptoms/ (accessed 11 January 2022).

NICE (2018) Post-Traumatic Stress Disorder: NICE Guidance. [online] Available at: www.nice.org.uk/guidance/NG116 (accessed 11 January 2022).

Office for National Statistics (2021) Deaths Involving COVID-19 in the Care Sector, England and Wales: Deaths Registered between Week Ending 20 March 2020 and Week Ending 2 April 2021. [online] Available at: www.ons.gov.uk/peoplepopulationandcommunity/birthsdeathsandmarriages/deaths/articles/deathsinvolvingcovid19inthecaresectorenglandandwales/deathsregisteredbetweenweekending20march2020andweekending2april2021 (accessed 11 January 2022).

Parliamentary Bills (2017) Public Authority (Accountability) Bill. [online] Available at: https://bills.parliament.uk/bills/1978/news (accessed 11 January 2022).

Pearlman, L A and Maclan, P (1995) Vicarious Traumatization: An Empirical Study of the Effects of Trauma Work on Trauma Therapists. *Professional Psychology: Research and Practice*, 26(6): 558–65.

Pittaway, E, Bartolomei, L and Rees, S (2004) Gendered Dimensions of the 2004 Tsunami and a Potential Social Work Response in Post-Disaster Situations. *International Social Work*, 50(3): 307–19.

Powles, L (2020) Are Men at Greater Risk from Covid-19? 30 November [online] Available at: www.bupa.co.uk/newsroom/ourviews/men-at-risk-covid19 (accessed 11 January 2022).

Public Health England (2020) Review of Disparities in Risks and Outcomes of Covid-19. [online] Available at: https://assets.publishing.service.gov.uk/government/uploads/system/uploads/attachment_data/file/908434/Disparities_in_the_risk_and_outcomes_of_COVID_August_2020_update.pdf (accessed 11 January 2022).

Quitangon, G and Evces, M R (2015) *Vicarious Trauma and Disaster Mental Health*. New York, NY: Routledge.

Reid, W (2020) Black Lives Matter: Social Work must Respond with Action – Not Platitudes. *Community Care*, 12 June. [online] Available at: www.communitycare.co.uk/2020/06/12/black-lives-matter-social-work-must-respond-action-platitudes/ (accessed 11 January 2022).

Romanou, E and Belton, E (2020) Isolated and Struggling: Social Isolation and the Risk of Child Maltreatment, in Lockdown and Beyond. NSPCC. [online] Available at: https://learning.nspcc.org.uk/media/2246/isolated-and-struggling-social-isolation-risk-child-maltreatment-lockdown-and-beyond.pdf (accessed 11 January 2022).

Roy, E A (2020) 'Kiwis – Go Home': New Zealand to go into Month-Long Lockdown to Fight Coronavirus. *Independent*, 23 March. [online] Available at: www.theguardian.com/world/2020/mar/23/kiwis-go-home-new-zealand-to-go-into-month-long-lockdown-to-fight-coronavirus (accessed 11 January 2022).

Ruch, G, Turney, D and Ward, A (2010) *Relationship-based Social Work: Getting to the Heart of Practice*. London: Jessica Kinsley.

SAMHSA (2014) SAMHSA'S Concept of Trauma and Guidance for a Trauma-Informed Approach. [online] Available at: https://ncsacw.samhsa.gov/userfiles/files/SAMHSA_Trauma.pdf (accessed 11 January 2022).

Saunders, J (2021) Manchester Arena Inquiry Volume 1: Security for the Arena. Report of the Public Inquiry into the Attack on Manchester Arena on 22nd May 2017. [online] Available at: https://files.manches terarenainquiry.org.uk/live/uploads/2021/06/17164904/CCS0321126 370-002_MAI-Report-Volume-ONE_WebAccessible.pdf (accessed 11 January 2022).

Seballos, F, Tanner, T, Tarazona, M and Gallegos, J (2011) Children and Disasters: Understanding Impact and Enabling Agency. [online] Available at: https://opendocs.ids.ac.uk/opendocs/bitstream/handle/20.500.12413/ 2367/Children%20and%20disasters.pdf?sequence=1andisAllowed=y (accessed 11 January 2022).

Sen, R, Kerr, C, MacIntyre, J, Featherstone, B, Gupta, A, and Quinn-Aziz, A (2021) Social Work under Covid-19: A Thematic Analysis of Articles in 'SW2020 under Covid-19 Magazine'. *The British Journal of Social Work*. doi:10.1093/bjsw/bcab094

Sommerlad, J (2019) Kegworth Air Disaster: What Happened and How Did the Plane Crash Change Airline Safety? *Independent*, 8 January. [online] Available at: www.independent.co.uk/news/uk/home-news/kegworth-air-disaster-30th-anniversary-boeing-midland-737-leicestershire-plane-crash-a8717656.html (accessed 11 January 2022).

Steinmetz, K (2020) She Coined the Term 'Intersectionality' Over 30 Years Ago. Here's What It Means to Her Today. *Time*, 20 February. [online] Available at: https://time.com/5786710/kimberle-crenshaw-intersectional ity/ (accessed 11 January 2022).

Stephenson, J and Weil, S (eds) (1992) *Quality in Learning: A Capability Approach in Higher Education*. London: Kegan Page.

Szistova, J and Pyles, L (2018) *Production of Disaster and Recovery in Post-earthquake Haiti: Disaster Industrial Complex*. Oxford: Routledge.

Townsend, M (2020) Revealed: Surge in Domestic Violence during Covid-19 Crisis. *The Guardian*, 12 April. [online] Available at: www.theguardian.com/society/2020/apr/12/domestic-violence-surges-seven-hundred-per-cent-uk-coronavirus (accessed 11 January 2022).

Tudor, R, Maidment, J, Campbell, A and Whittaker, K (2015) Examining the Role of Craft in Post-Earthquake Recovery: Implications for Social Work Practice. *British Journal of Social Work*, 45(1): 205–20.

Turner, A (2020) Most Social Workers Say Covid-19 Has Negatively Hit their Work and the Lives of Those They Support. *Community Care*, May 28. [online] Available at: www.communitycare.co.uk/2020/05/28/social-workers-say-coronavirus-negatively-affected-services-people-they-support/ (accessed 11 January 2022).

UK Government (2020a) Prime Minister's Statement on Coronavirus (Covid-19): 12 March 2020. [online] Available at: www.gov.uk/government/speeches/pm-statement-on-coronavirus-12-march-2020 (accessed 11 January 2022).

UK Government (2020b) Prime Minister's Statement on Coronavirus (Covid-19): 17 March 2020. [online] Available at: www.gov.uk/government/speeches/pm-statement-on-coronavirus-17-march-2020 (accessed 11 January 2022).

UK Government (2020c) Prime Minister's Statement on Coronavirus (Covid-19): 23 March 2020. [online] Available at: www.gov.uk/government/speeches/pm-address-to-the-nation-on-coronavirus-23-march-2020 (accessed 11 January 2022).

UK Parliament (2021) The Adoption and Children (Coronavirus) (Amendment) Regulations. [online] Available at: https://commonslibrary.parliament.uk/research-briefings/cbp-8934/ (accessed 11 January 2022).

UNESCO (2020) COVID-19-Related Discrimination and Stigma: A Global Phenomenon? [online] Available at: https://en.unesco.org/news/covid-19-related-discrimination-and-stigma-global-phenomenon (accessed 11 January 2022).

University of Durham and BASW (2021) *Social Work during COVID-19: Learning for the Future*. Birmingham: BASW.

WHO (2020a) WHO Director-General's Remarks at the Media Briefing on 2019-CoV on 11 February 2020. [online] Available at: www.who.int/director-general/speeches/detail/who-director-general-s-remarks-at-the-media-briefing-on-2019-ncov-on-11-february-2020 (accessed 11 January 2022).

WHO (2020b) Munich Security Conference. 15 February. [online] Available at: www.who.int/director-general/speeches/detail/munich-security-conference (accessed 11 January 2022).

WHO (2020c) WHO Director-General's Opening Remarks at the Media Briefing on Covid-19. 11 March. [online] Available at: www.who.int/director-general/speeches/detail/who-director-general-s-opening-remarks-at-the-media-briefing-on-covid-19---11-march-2020 (accessed 11 January 2022).

WHO (2020d) Mental Health and Psychosocial Considerations during the Covid-19 Outbreak. 18 March [online] Available at: www.who.int/publications/i/item/WHO-2019-nCoV-MentalHealth-2020.1 (accessed 11 January 2022).

WHO (2020e) World Health Organization. [online] Available at: www.who.int/hac/about/definitions/en/ (accessed 11 January 2022).

WHO (2020f) Covid Preparedness, Readiness and Response Actions for Covid-19. 4 November [online] Available at: https://apps.who.int/iris/bitstream/handle/10665/336373/WHO-COVID-19-Community_Actions-2020.5-eng.pdf (accessed 11 January 2022).

WHO (2020g) Listings of WHO's Response to COVID-19. 29 June. [online] Available at: https://www.who.int/news/item/29-06-2020-covidtimeline

Willett, J (2019) Micro Disasters: Expanding the Social Work Conceptualization of Disasters. *International Social Work*, 62(1): 133–45.

Willow, C (2020) Court of Appeal Rules Education Secretary Acted Unlawfully in Removing Safeguards for Children in Care. [online] Available at: https://article39.org.uk/2020/11/24/court-of-appeal-rules-education-secretary-acted-unlawfully-in-removing-safeguards-for-children-in-care/ (accessed 11 January 2022).

Wirral Ark (2020) 'Everyone In' Showed We Can End Homelessness. We Need to Build on this Good Work. 26 June. [online] Available at: https://wirralark.org.uk/end-homelessness/ (accessed 11 January 2022).

Worldometer (nd) Covid-19 Coronavirus Pandemic. [online] Available at: www.worldometers.info/coronavirus/ (accessed 11 January 2022).

Yanay, U and Benjamin, B (2005) The Role of Social Workers in Disasters: The Jerusalem Experience. *International Social Work*, 48(3): 263–76.

Index

Press Council, 126
professional capabilities, 92
Professional Capabilities Framework
    (PCF), 10, 90–2, 104
professional impacts of helping
    professionals, 108, 113
professional unpreparedness, during
    Covid-19 pandemic, 22–3
prolonged grief disorder
    (ICD-11), 109
protective security for venues
    after Manchester Arena
    bombing, 123
psychiatric injury claims and
    Hillsborough tragedy, 122
psychosocial interventions, 20
psychosocial support to
    practitioners, 101
Public Authority (Accountability)
    Bill, 121
Public Health England, 87, 89, 95
purpose, as help through difficult
    time, 39–40

Reach, 126
realpolitik, 20
Rebuilding People's Lives After
    Disasters (RIPL), 18
recovery and time limitation, 112
Red Cross, The, 3
reflective space, 117
relationship-based practice, 101
remote technologies as support
    resource, 19
resources, wastage of, 19
responding, need-based, 68
retraumatisation, 65, 120

safe practices, 69, 70
safe space for social workers, 117
Saunders, Sir John, 54
secondary trauma, 117
self-care, 9, 81, 110
self-help resources, 24
sensitivity, 70
Serious Case Reviews, 121
shared experience, 116
shared traumatic reality, 108, 116
Smallman, Nicole, murder of, 8
social context
    of disasters, 7–9
    of post-traumatic growth, 109
social disparities during Covid-19
    pandemic, 94
social injustice, 94–5
social isolation and children
    abuse, 96
social justice, 92, 112
social media, 94, 97, 124, 128
social work
    definition of, 90
    in disasters, 5–6
    education of, 2
    future of, 128–30
    invisibility of, 18–21
    reframing roles of, 21–2
social work responses, 50
    to Covid-19 pandemic, 23–7
    to Grenfell Tower fire disaster,
        45–6, 78–9
    preparedness in, 71
    and sensitivity, 70
social workers
    accountability of, 63, 65, 70, 121
    being in control, 55